^A CATHOLIC SURVIVAL GUIDE

A CATHOLIC SURVIVAL GUIDE

PLAIN TALK FROM THE PEWS: PROTECTING FAMILY AND FAITH

ANDREW P. HICKS, PH.D.
MACK R. HICKS, PH.D.

Splenium House Press

Published By:
Splenium House Press

ISBN Paperback: 978-0-9712587-4-7
ISBN Hardcover: 978-0-9712587-8-5
ISBN eBook (Kindle): 978-0-9712587-6-1
ISBN eBook: (ePub): 978-0-9712587-7-8

Library of Congress Control Number: 2019902606

Names: Hicks, Andrew P. and Hicks, Mack R.
Title: A Catholic Survival Guide: (Plain Talk from the Pews: Protecting Family and Faith) 217 pages, 246KB.
Identifiers: LCCN: ISBN:
Subjects: Jesus, Religion, Faith, Christian, Psychology, Catholic, Science, Research, Sermons, Holy Spirit, Probability, Sex-Scandal, Hysteria, Gender, Charity, Priests, Shroud, Mass, Polls, Millenniums.

Cover and Interior Design: Creative Publishing Book Design.

Manufactured in the U.S.A.

DEDICATED TO DEFENDERS OF THE FAITH:

St. Justin Martyr, St. Peter, St. Francis of Assisi, St. Catherine of Siena, St. Anthony of Padua, St. Paul, St. Mary, St. Augustine, St. Cecilia, St. John Chrysostom, St. Theresa of Avila, St. Sebastian, St. Padre Pio, St. Bernadette, St. Monica, Thomas Aquinas, Dietrich Bonhoeffer, St. Maximillian Kolbe, St. John Paul II, St. Pope Pius XII, Rev. Billy Graham, St. Mother Theresa, St. Joseph, St. Jude Thaddeus, St. Clare, St. Theresa of Calcutta, St. Benedict, St. Agnes, St. Lucy, St. Sophia, St. James, St. Philip, St. Andrew.

Table of Contents

PART ONE
An Insider's Guide For People in the Pews

PART TWO
Psychology and Religion. Who Are Our Church Leaders? Can They Help Us Now?

PART THREE
Can Modern Science *Prove* that Church Origins Were Inspired?

PART FOUR
Do Church Teachings Reflect Characteristics of the Brain and Central Nervous System?

PART FIVE
The Devil's Laboratory: Media and Pop Psychology

PART SIX
Undressing the Devil

PART SEVEN
Inoculation—"God is Dead," Gay Marriage, Abortion

PART EIGHT
Summing Up

Preface:
Mike's Complaints

Mike Elliot enjoys a good life, or at least a pleasant one, but some things are beginning to bother him, even keep him awake at night. There are rumors that the discount store he manages may close some of its locations. His wife Kathy's job at the local newspaper is always in jeopardy. In the past, Mike has relied on his family and his faith to see them through tough times.

But times seem to be changing. His daughter, who is a freshman in college, says her sociology professor thinks the life of Jesus is just a myth, and that most Christians have stopped going to church. Mike's son, a freshman in high school, wants to spend some weekends at a Christian Youth Camp. "They're really nice people," his son says, and Mike knows that. Will his son's faith in the Catholic Church be weakened?

One of his best friend's daughters is divorced and some other Catholic young people are living together. If they do eventually marry, they talk about having their weddings at a beach resort instead of at their Church—or any church.

The local newspaper is still bringing up the priest sex abuse scandals. The day after a well-known TV host was accused of sexual harassment, the newspaper showed a picture of Pope Francis shaking hands with the man. Mike shook his head. "There was the Pope, right there in his white vestments, signifying purity, smiling and giving a trusting handshake to this guy." (As it turns out, the brief meeting was long before these alleged incidents were publicized).

"Where is all of this going?" Mike wonders. He talked to his priest and that helped, but news stories and research findings just seem to be piling up against his faith. He knows that newspapers may be biased, and not always accurate, but what's a person to believe anymore? He'll keep praying, but he sure could use a little help about now.

The authors of *A Catholic Survival Guide* hope to supply some answers for Mike and other Catholics in the pews who are struggling with many unfortunate changes within our western culture. We intend to do this through clear and straight-forward language and some insiders' knowledge of the Church of Rome.

Please join us.

Introduction

We thought the best way to help our friend Mike, whose worrisome time was detailed in the *Preface,* was to write an honest, straightforward book for Catholics in the pews. Most publishers don't think this is a good idea, because they believe the average person doesn't read that much, and they have to stay in business. They may be right, but we believed this book needed to be written.

No, to be greeted with open arms by publishers, we would need to write something for our extremely well-educated Catholic leaders who like to use Latin and Greek and enjoy debating profound philosophical questions, or at least doctors, lawyers, and Indian chiefs. Folks with graduate degrees in religion who can understand the complex dogma of the church. But guess what? Christ didn't have much time for such things. He was a hard-working construction guy from a little burg who liked blue-collar fisherman and farmers. And besides that, the Catholic Catechism is pretty darn clear and unsophisticated. Just tells it like it is.

You might wonder if we know what people in the pews really think, but we fit right in. We have some advanced degrees, but we are just plain old pew people like everyone else.

Some of our non-Catholic friends go to church to listen to inspiring sermons, and that's all well and good, but listening to dry words instead of immersing oneself in all the mysterious gifts of the Holy Spirit, seems just that—kind of dry. It's almost a denial of the Holy Spirit, who is in our presence now. Just hearing about the interventions of the Holy Ghost 10,000 years ago isn't the same as acknowledging his presence in our adoration and daily lives today. The Holy Spirit, or the forgotten spirit? Listening or immersing? You decide.

And some young folks look for really cool churches that fit their own life styles and personalities, a place where they can meet other cool kids. And some are looking for exotic, spiritual experiences—something more than hum-drum stuff. But we think they're missing out, big time. One analogy is jumping off a ten-foot-high diving board into a swimming pool. It seems awfully high up there—and scary. Maybe crawl down the ladder one ring at a time and then stick a toe in? How sensible, but how weak and boring.

We're suggesting you take the big jump and make a huge splash so you can feel, smell, taste and experience the mother of all Christianity. If you want spiritual and exotic, we've got that big time. If you like Halloween and spook shows, we've got the granddaddy of all spooks—the Holy Ghost. And more: we've got relics (body parts), art, sculpture, incense, candles, exorcism, music, singing, paintings, Technicolor windows, and speaking in tongues. And don't forget Holy Bread, manna baked in heaven. All ways for the Spirit to touch us and move us.

Instead of just listening to well-meaning speakers who will entertain you and make you feel great for an hour or two, or going to the haunted house at Universal Studios, come and meet the crazies at your local Catholic Church. Rednecks, rich folks, and everything in-between. And you might want to travel around the world to visit mighty Catholic cathedrals. Go to the Vatican and see the pope. Be sure to give him our best.

Crazy all right, but at the same time who are the most intelligent and best balanced folks we know? How about members of the U.S. Supreme Court? Guess which Christian denomination has the most folks on the court? Yep, those creative Catholics with their lurking Holy Spirit. How can that be? Think about it. And who's the biggest? ("We're #1, yeah!") and oldest Christian church (2000 years). And let's not forget the most charitable church in the world. No one gives more to the poor than we do.

We must have gotten a few things right.

So why doesn't everyone flock to the Church? They do in some parts of the world, but not so much lately in our western culture. We think some folks are scared off because of all the stimulation the church offers. It can be seen as overwhelming. It's jumping right in rather than taking a picture of the swimming pool, or a selfie while sitting safely on the sidelines. All those rules and prayer books and rosaries and candles. Just too much going on they think, without really thinking. There's a fear of getting lost in there, too, maybe stuck, like quicksand, and not getting out. Just being smothered by it all.

But some Catholics have left the church and then returned only to leave again and return again. Just like some folks at the time of Jesus. No, you can walk away at any time. You're free. People make this mistake with their doctors, too. You'll hear them say the doctor ordered them to do such and such and they had to do it. Well surprise, the doctors works for you. They're your employees, in a sense. The doc's usually right, but you have choices. Here's an experiment for you. Go to a Mass, sit in the back row and leave after ten minutes. Just walk out! No lightning bolts, we promise. And no one going tsk, tsk, tsk, either.

Of course it seems cleaner and a lot, lot easier to just experience Jesus directly. To be born again —without any rigmarole. Who needs to deal with the bureaucrats when you can go straight to the boss? Halleluiah! And you get to keep it a secret, because it's no one else's business in the first place. But Jesus started the Church. It's the best way to know him.

We think some of these fears and concerns come from childhood, when things were often overwhelming. But now you've grown up. Now you can choose to hitchhike down life's highway on your own, feeling proud and important, despite your slow and erratic pace, or accept a first-class ticket on Air Force One—all the way to heaven.

So think about it. Give it a chance. It could be the big payoff.

Getting back to Mike's complaints, changes in our culture are making lots of Christians nervous. Criticism comes from non-religious people who feel sure that they can just rely on their own good judgement, along with scientific progress, to eliminate the need for religion, especially a religion with long-standing rituals and concepts.

Who needs religion when science makes mind-bending progress every day without it? Here's a message on a London double-decker bus: "There's probably no God. Now stop worrying and enjoy your life." My, it must be great to feel so free and easy about everything.

In the 1950's the Catholic Church was in its heyday in the United States. In his 2016 book, *Getting Religion,* Ken Woodward wrote about how things have changed. Looking back, he says that baby boomers were looking for a religion that had nothing to do with old texts, or institutions. Instead, they wanted the experience of *themselves* as sacred. And some millennials don't readily identify with any institutions—political, civic, academic, or religious.[1]

Ross Douthat also agrees that things have changed: Those preaching self-fulfillment have done away with original sin and the result is "a society where pride becomes healthy self-esteem, vanity becomes self-improvement, adultery becomes following your heart, and greed and gluttony become living the American dream."[2]

In the movie, "Concussion," a National Football League doctor pointed out the power of the NFL. "We own the day (Sunday) of the week. It used to be the day for church."[3]

In 1965, over 80% of entering college students reported that a meaningful philosophy of life was essential or very important, and fewer than 40% said being well off financially was most important. Now these figures are reversed.[4]

For two years, Nancy Jo Sales researched the use of social media by teenage girls and concluded that teens use their Smartphones for "bonding, bullying—and texting naked pictures. Lots and lots of naked pictures."[5]

Of course, the authors of this book have worked with kids and families, and we aren't shocked by immature behavior, wherever it is found. Let's face it, we all need structure and religious values—adults as well as kids. It's easy to give in to the "commandments" of a secular (secular meaning worldly and irreligious) culture, and never before has a culture tempted every living soul with such a bombardment of sleazy and disheartening news and entertainment.

Most books today aren't written in our everyday way of speaking and writing and don't deal with research or media bias. Authors of most other books don't examine scientific claims because they aren't scientists themselves. We are, and that's what makes us different. We want to show how research is used (and misused) to attack the Church and how good research supports Church teachings. We will also help the reader spot bad research and biased media.

Before we go any further, perhaps we should introduce the people in the pews who wrote this book. We authors are a father and son team. We're not journalists, we're not academics, and we didn't have the fortitude or calling for the clergy. But we have conducted evaluations of priesthood candidates for over 35 years.

Ours is a down-to-earth reading of the Catholic Church. Two psychologists share their views on the Church's beliefs and practices. How does the church stand up to modern research and media bias? Is the church responding to our everyday needs as we now know them, or is it operating in the dark ages? Stay tuned.

So, if you are a Catholic who feels discouraged because of our culture and the role science and the media play in it, or have fallen away from the Church or Christianity in general and want to take another look, you've come to the right place. Maybe you're a skeptic, an agnostic, or just a churchgoer in the pews who wants some straight talk on the universal Catholic Church and its incredible history.

We present our case in a zestful manner, with occasional humor and more than a few politically incorrect observations. So bring your prayer book, a pair of comfortable shoes, and a good flashlight. Poke around inside the greatest God-made institution on earth.

PART ONE

**An Insider's Guide
For People in the Pews**

Chapter 1

An insider's view of the Mass. Want to sneak into a Roman Catholic Mass and spy on the secret rites of the papal zealots?

No, we're not members of a subversive group, but there are lingering suspicions about the Catholic Church in our country, possibly because of the massive immigration of Irish to our shores in the late 19th century and our Church's reverence for the pope.

A Florida psychologist told one of the authors about his childhood in a small town in the center of the state. He said he and his fellow teenagers were "bored out of their minds" and found only three interesting things to do in their town: "You could hide at the back of the cemetery and play eerie music to scare people parked in a nearby Lovers' Lane, "watch haircuts" over at the barber shop, or park down the street from the only Catholic family in town, and watch them hang out their wash." Yep, those Catholics had to be strange ones, alright.

Before we take a tour of the Mass, let's look at the word itself. Leave it to Catholics to use a foreign sounding term to describe their religious services. Other folks just say they're going to church, but no, Catholics have to have a mysterious name for what they do. Could it be a demonic code-word devised by the Vatican? No, it's nothing quite so creative or intriguing. The word "Mass" simply comes from the final words of the Mass as spoken in Latin: "Ite, Missa Est.," go, it is dismissed.

Here are some other names found in our Church, supplied by D. Withers: Pews: "A medieval torture device still found in Catholic Churches." Relics: "People who have gone to Mass for so long, they actually know when to sit, kneel, and stand." Incense: "Holy smoke!"

With those serious definitions out of the way, we're ready for Mass. *Trip Advisor* might warn you about church parking and award only three stars for the whole experience, but let's give it a try, anyway. A Sunday Mass at 10:00 or 11:00 AM is often the best attended Mass of the week. There is usually a parking lot adjacent to the church and most drivers are quite courteous.

It's after Mass that you should be concerned for your life, because a few of these folks seem to have been energized by the sermon and are impatient to hit the road and spread the faith—or get home to watch a football game or soccer match on TV. Maybe they've already forgotten what they learned in church, even though remembering the good word for 5 or 10 minutes shouldn't be that tough. Oh well—there's that Catholic Church of sinners thing again!

When you get to the front door, just walk straight into the entrance or lobby. The Church has another old-world name for this area. It's called the Narthex. You won't see any signs that say "Narthex." We doubt that most Catholics can tell you what the word means. Anyway, it's just inside the church entrance. You may see people dipping their fingers in a basin of water and making the sign of the cross. This old German tradition of signing oneself with water blessed by a priest is a nice way to both begin and end the Mass.

Where did the sign of the cross come from? No, it's not a secret symbol used to ward off Dracula or the I.R.S. Ancient Hebrews traced the last letters of the Hebrew alphabet on their foreheads as a sign of hope, but the Catholic version developed independent of Jewish tradition. The philosopher Plato described a giant + written upon the universe, while Justin Martyr, the saint this book is dedicated to, believed the symbol of the cross was embedded in all things human. To Catholics, the cross symbolizes the crucifix. And don't mistake it as simply an emblem of the Catholic Church, sort of like the Rotary Club Wheel. No, it's a symbol of hope in God's promise to redeem us . . . and it's really cool.[1]

Find a pew and sit down. Most parishioners will genuflect in the aisle, touching one knee to the floor, a symbol of piety and reverence, before entering a pew. Once in the pew, they will kneel and then, after a short prayer, sit back. As a visitor, you can ignore all of that; you don't need to worry about standing, sitting, kneeling etc. as the Mass progresses.

Despite the rumors of cramped, musty churches stuffed with statues of saints, you'll usually find a beautiful, open, well-lighted church, with stained-glass windows, fresh flowers, and possibly statues of Jesus, Mary, and a saint or two. Some parishioners light candles for their loved ones, alive or deceased. It's neat to see these candles flickering inside their glass containers. "Christ, the light of the world."

Lighting candles can be traced to classical Greece and Biblical Judaism. By lighting a candle of devotion, "you offer your prayers to

God and join your brothers and sisters of the historical Church in active petition and thanksgiving."[2] Sociologist Rodney Stark, who we will discuss later, observed that people who call themselves secular (meaning worldly and irreligious) humanists, are really letting us know they aren't keen about conventional brands of faith. They are more likely to show an interest in cutting edge, mystical, and magical approaches. That should put the Catholic Church in a pretty good place when you think about the format of our service: lighted candles, incense and belief in the Holy Spirit!

The cross, sometimes life-size or larger, is usually found over or near the main altar. If there's no crucifix dominating the landscape, you aren't in a real Catholic Church.

The format of the service (called the liturgy) is fairly straightforward and is always the same. There are general prayers followed by readings from the Old Testament, along with St. Paul or the apostles, and of course the words of Jesus from the New Testament. This is followed by the homily (sermon).

During the Mass, there are four or five hymns that tie in with the readings for that day. After the readings, everyone says the "Our Father." The priest blesses the bread and wine, and lines form. You can just sit tight and no one will think anything of it. If you want, you can get in line and cross your arms over your chest for a blessing from the priest.

The altar boys and girls are marvelous, especially the tiny six-year-olds. Wearing their black and white blouses and cassocks, they follow the lead of older servers, usually their older siblings. We keep waiting for them to drop the gold cross or spill the wine brought to the altar for blessing and communion, but they bravely carry on and bring a smile to the faces of adult parishioners.

You'll see some interesting people in most parishes. We like churches that are not in a ritzy part of town because all types of people attend, making it catholic (universal) as well as Catholic. We have yet to see tattoos. Maybe St. Paul's warning that the body should be a temple of purity and virtue has made its invisible mark. Here you'll find sinners without tattoos—or maybe the tattoos are tucked away under their clothes.

Parishioners are evenly divided between men and women and their dress is usually casual. Some wear a nice shirt and long pants or skirt, but we also see T-shirts identifying a resort, a college, or an athletic team, especially in tourist-happy Florida.

Recently, we watched a pretty gal wearing an outfit made up of very tight, short shorts, torn blue jeans, and cowboy boots. Our first thought was "oh my God! She's going to help dispense communion,"—how inappropriate and irreverent. However, this was quickly followed by the thought that if she means well, although a bit unaware, we're happy to have her here with the rest of us imperfect people. Back in the 50's a nun would have stood by to advise her not to unintentionally become "an occasion of sin."

Yep, the Catholic Church stretches out its arms to all comers. You will see wheelchairs, walkers and canes, along with autistic, psychotic, hyperactive, and intellectually limited kids and adults, sitting alongside doctors, lawyers and business folks. At a recent mass, one man leaned his head against a large pillar at the front of the church during the blessing of the bread and wine; another man raised his arms hallelujah style. His partner had to gently push each arm down or his arms might have stayed frozen in midair until the end of the Mass. Over to the left, two well-dressed gay gentlemen had bemused expressions on their faces.

We were at the 12:10 weekday Mass at St. Mary's church in St. Petersburg, Florida not too long ago, along with about 40 other parishioners. We couldn't help but see a giant of a man, about eight pews ahead of us, who had to be 6'7" tall and whose weight would best be measured in tonnage. In his 60s, dressed completely in black, with silver white hair, he had to rest his left leg in the main aisle because of his size. We thought he had probably played offensive lineman on a pro football team.

When the priest said it was time for the sign of peace, this man-mountain didn't just wave at the folks around him. Instead, he unscrambled his barrel-sized legs and ambled across the main aisle to shake hands with a twenty-something black man who was a six-footer, and possibly an athlete himself. The giant then turned and shook hands with a female college student, sitting three pews behind the black man who sported a long pigtail. Yes, black lives do matter, and college coeds' lives do matter and ex-football players' lives do matter. Welcome to the Catholic, catholic (universal) Church.

At one Mass, on Pentecost Sunday, we saw a well-dressed man sitting in the third pew, near the altar, extending his arms to copy the priest's movements. Then we noticed a small Terrier dog on his lap. Would the priest tolerate a dog attending this Holy Service? Perhaps the dog was therapeutic, we thought. Then, to our astonishment, the strange man left his little friend in order to usher people to communion. We couldn't see where he left his blessed pet in the pew and hoped the diminutive pooch didn't decide to make a run for it. Alas, all was well. The man completed his task and returned to his pew without incident.

Another time, on the feast of Saint Francis of Assisi, the patron saint of animals, we turned to give other parishioners the sign of peace, but were greeted by two folks in the back pew who held up the paws of their two white fluffy dogs to give their greetings. Hey, this is fun! No doubt, Saint Francis was smiling.

At one Sunday Mass, a poor family with four children sat in a pew near the altar. The youngest boy, about seven, was spinning like a whirling dervish between hops and shutters. We immediately diagnosed him as suffering from clinical hyperactivity. Good thing we two doctors were present to assess the situation. Maybe we could help. The child's mother, however, had a different idea, and took him to the bathroom. When the boy returned, he appeared to be cured and our diagnosis had to be changed from "attention deficit disorder with hyperactivity" to "needing a bathroom break." By the way, Catholics not only tolerate families with young children, they welcome them. Not all that stuck up, are we?

Before a noon Mass, a friend of ours helped a wheelchair-bound young man, with what she described as an angelic face, by lighting some candles for him because he was unable to access the elevated candle area, in front of the statue of Mary. When she next saw him, he presented her with a beautiful rosary he had hand-carved. Acts of mercy? No, just the love of God—and a new friend.

Watch the faces of parishioners returning to their pews after receiving the bread and wine. You'll see mostly reverent expressions, but also a few joyful, blank, distracted, and nonchalant ones. After receiving a blessing, instead of Communion, because they have not yet made their first communion, some younger children may skip back to their pews, oblivious of it all. But no one looks angry, and that's a very good thing.

What about music? We will tell you about one piece of music you probably won't hear during your next visit to a Catholic Church,

Christopher Theofanidis' Rainbow Body. This symphony is one of the most frequently performed orchestral pieces by a living world composer today. Theofanidis based his work on Catholic chants written by the *12th-century* German Benedictine Abbess, mystic Hildegard von Bingen. The name of her chant is Maria, O Auctrix Vite (Hail Mary, Source of Life).[3]

Aren't we lucky to have such a dramatic and inspiring church history? If you're a liberal Catholic and wants some really modern, hip music, we sometimes play Martin Luther's 1500's work, "A Mighty Fortress is Our God." More proof that our church can be flexible and stay up with the times! Ha.

You will hear other historical pieces, such as the African-American spiritual "Were You There?"[4] and of course pop sounding tunes such as Amazing Grace. As long as the primary singer isn't too screechy, these beautiful songs and chants add much to the Mass. There is often a rock and roll flavored musical group once each week, geared toward teens.

One Catholic Church in Indiana came up with an idea to raise money. At a parish fundraiser and auction for the school, someone paid several hundred dollars for the right to ban any song used at a Mass for an entire year. The winner chose to ban the song "Gather Us In." It's obvious that the pastor and the director of music had a sense of fun, as did those who were bidding for the "prize."

At the end of the service, it's best to wait until the priest leaves the altar and is out of sight before you get up to leave. A few folks will dart out early, perhaps to warm up their cars for the Indy 500 taking place in the parking lot. You don't need to talk to the priest, who will be waiting to greet parishioners near the exit or just outside, but if you feel like it, stop and say hello or give him a "God Bless" as you go by.

That's it. You may notice that you now feel a little better, maybe lighter. Tell your friends, have a good day, and please come again!

Chapter 2

Ho-hum sermons and old-hat scripture readings. (Copy this chapter for a clergy friend.)

Let's face it, hearing the same scripture readings over and over can be distracting and even boring. Sermons (now called homilies) are an important part of the Mass, but they can also interrupt the spiritual flow of the service if they are dry, boring, and lengthy. We have not conducted a scientific study of sermons, but psychological research, theory, and practice give us some usable guidelines.

If you're looking for a fiery, motivational speech, you won't usually find it at a Catholic Mass, unless it's during a special mission, which may happen a couple of times a year. Remember, the Catholic Mass is about Christ's sacrifice, which is repeated in the miracle of the bread and wine, not quite as much about *The Word*. That's why Catholics, unlike some folks in other communities, are less likely to go from church to church shopping for a pastor who is a dynamic speaker.

Bad homilies don't help us folks in the pews understand as much as they help the priest improve his lecturing skills. In other words, sometimes the priest focuses less on who is receiving the message and more on himself, the sender of the message. When we authors write reports, and as psychologists we write reports to parents, physicians, psychologists, psychiatrists, pediatricians, etc., our reports have to be different, because they keep the reader in mind and are not used as a way of showing how smart we are or how great our vocabulary is.

While our people in the pews are bright and capable, our priests sometimes forget that only about 30% of Americans have completed college. Our Church should represent most people; most parishioners didn't major in English literature or attend graduate school either! A monsignor, who was comfortable with all levels of society, gave very brief homilies during his children's Masses. He said this was because children had short attention spans, but then added: "so do many of their parents."

Here's an example of a sermon that is more like a lecture. "My observations entail the actualization within me of potential for knowledge, and thus a change of causation." Huh? Come again? Here's even worse stuff: clichés. "To rise with Christ we must die with Christ," "wages of sin," "anointing with scared chrism." Please raise your hand if you can define the word *chrism*.

The late Thomas Merton criticized some popular preachers who claimed you couldn't open the Bible without being "instantly subject to various supernatural jolts, shocks, short circuits, mystical feedback, and heaven knows what else besides." According to Merton, much more common reactions are "boredom, mystification, a sense that one has suddenly got lost, and even the onset of sleep."[1]

According to Merton, the saintly Dietrich Bonhoeffer, a Lutheran minister, frankly admitted his difficulty staying focused, even at a time when he was facing death in prison. Merton believed we shouldn't feel guilty if we are not instantly impressed with the Bible. He advised us to question passages in the Bible much as an unbeliever might, and he thought we should "experience it" rather than just read it.

This reminds us of a corny and slightly irreverent joke. It seems that a minister, who was indeed giving an hour long fiery speech, thundered against alcohol as a work of the devil. He demanded that parishioners take any alcohol they possessed, cart it down to the river, and throw it in! "Throw it all in the river," he ordered them. After the sermon, the massive choir, along with accompanying trumpets, began to play. "Shall We Gather at the River?"

So what do we need for a good sermon?

The best sermons usually involve the priest disclosing some of his own personal experiences. It really helps if the priest reveals something about himself, usually through a story about his own life as an adult or child. It could also incorporate a plot from a movie, a cartoon, or the experiences of a sports figure, actor, etc. This takes time, effort, reflection, creativity—and humility.

The reason priests sometimes give long abstract sermons, full of popular clichés, is that it is easy, and they are busy with other parish duties. Yes, it's rolling off a log compared to creating something new, something that relates to the real world, and makes us think about our own lives.

Some priests start out with an original, interesting, approach, sometimes a joke, but then switch to abstract ideas and clichés, like they're lecturing a college class. This isn't supposed to be a lecture. It's the word of God made clear, understandable, and fascinating. It's easy to spot parishioners who become distracted, because they will do things like reading the church newsletter precisely when the priest switches gears and goes to safe but mundane lecturing.

This should be valuable feedback for the priest, but some priests just don't see it. What, for God's sake are they looking at, if they can't see the faces of people in the pews who are only 30 feet away? People with vacant eyes who are being polite, bless them. If they aren't keeping the attention of most folks in the pews, then they need to change their sermon, pronto.

The sermon should relate the main message of the readings and repeat a helpful point two or three times over the course of the six-to-eight-minute sermon. If we graded our priests' homilies, we'd give most of them an A for *reading and talking about* what was said in the gospel (the same things we've heard before—over and over), but we'd have to give them a D for *why and how*. Why is this important now and how do we really apply it to our lives? Don't just give us clichés like "go out and help people," or "realize that God is big and we are small."

Sometimes less is more. Psychological studies show that a lot of talking, after initial ideas are presented, may actually interfere with remembering those initial concepts. When you visit your physician's office and she's wondering if your memory is slipping, she may read you some names or a list of items, but she will not ask you to repeat them until the end of your visit. She realizes that additional conversation and time delay interfere with your memory.

So it's ironic that when a priest adds more and more verbiage, they may actually be interfering with the parishioner's ability to remember the original and more heartfelt ideas. (Tell this to your priest but don't tell him you got this idea from us. Ha!)

The best method is the one used by Jesus when he was on earth, and that was the parable. It is simply a colorful story, usually one we can picture in our minds, such as a seed falling to the ground. The tiny seed is insignificant and hardly noticeable, but when it dies, the result is a gigantic tree offering shade and nourishment for many.

Yes, priests give long sermons because they are easier than short ones. U.S. President Woodrow Wilson was once asked if he would give a talk; he wanted to know how long it would be. He said if it was a five-minute talk he needed two days to prepare. If it was a 20-minute talk he needed a day to prepare. If it was an hour-long speech, he could begin immediately.

If the priest wants the parishioners in the pews to walk away and remember what was said, eight minutes is about the maximum time for an effective sermon. Short homilies also avoid boredom, staring into space, falling asleep, and narcolepsy. If the priest can't remember the length of the sermon as he goes along, he might set a cell phone alarm on vibrate mode for seven minutes and give himself a minute to wrap things up. Better yet, he should use the phone to snap a picture of sleeping parishioners. One priest likes to ask a parishioner to volunteer to time the sermon to make sure he finishes in a reasonable time.

If the priest sums up the sermon by tying everything together in the conclusion, this helps solidify it within the brain's memory bank, but if the sermon exceeds about eight minutes, even excellent ones lose their impact.

So it's pretty simple and doesn't take an Einstein to know that it should be a parable-like talk that one can easily visualize, is interesting and includes real-world experiences that we can link to the readings for our current time and culture, not 2000 years ago. Otherwise, we are pretending that living conditions 2000 years ago were identical to today's living conditions, and this interferes with our understanding of the meaning of the readings.

The above recommendations are based on a long history of learning theory and laboratory research. When we give a talk or write a report, it is easy to focus on ourselves rather than the listener or reader. We all have big egos. This is part of what religion tries to help us to correct.

Psychological research shows that stories are far superior to dry facts when we want something to stick in our memory banks. Stories make us think. So the next time you find yourself drifting off during a reading or homily (sermon), get active! Delve into the subject matter, ask yourself questions, and apply it to your own life experiences or stories you've read.

Sometimes priests are guilty of dry repetition because they are burned out, stressed, or just plain tired. Yes, priests are human and fully capable of fatigue and stress.

One of this book's authors returned from a trip to Italy and told his pastor he had heard a great sermon in Naples. The pastor said, "I didn't realize you understood Italian" and the author answered, "I don't." This was said in jest, but perhaps it gave this priest something to think about; more of that darn Catholic humor!

Chapter 3

Should doubters still go to church? What if you're lukewarm about going to church or have more important things to do? Here is *The Workingman's Guide to Church-Going.* (Copy it and give it to a lazy Catholic or non-believer.)

Good Reasons Not To Go To Church:

"It's Groundhog Day and the groundhog didn't see his shadow."

"I can make up my own mind about what's right and wrong. I don't need some holier-than-thou stranger telling me how to live and making me feel guilty."

"I don't want to be a hypocrite, like some folks I know, who go to church but don't seem any better for it. I wouldn't buy a used car from a couple of these folks."

"I don't want to sit in church and have others think I'm stupid for being there."

"My parents went to church now and then, but I never paid much attention and they didn't seem happier than most other folks. I don't know what good it did them."

"If there is a God, he must not care about the people he made, because bad things happen to people all the time, and praying won't change that."

"Church-goers can't prove God exists. Neither can scientists."

"When I'm at church, I might miss fishing, golfing, or a football or baseball playoff game on TV."

"The people at church seem nice, but I just don't feel anything when I'm there."

"If I make a commitment, I'll feel trapped and smothered. Won't be able to get out—and they'll want my money."

Good Reasons To Go To Church:

In the early days of the Church, people thought highly of Christians because of their kindness and values. They still do.

If you want to stay physically healthy, research shows that attendance at church is a powerful predictor of physical health.[1]

You're enjoying the privileges of America, and it was built on faith and hope. "In God we trust."

Employers feel good about churchgoers because they are usually honest, hard-working, and trustworthy.

Your parents, spouse, and children will be proud of you and not have to be embarrassed about defending you when their friends ask why you're not in church. Your kids may feel you're letting them down.

You might learn something bigger than auto-racing or the World Series. Did you know that Jesus was built like an NFL linebacker?

Hauling trees makes for a powerful physique. And he skipped college because he had to work. If you could play soccer with Jesus and share a beer, what would you think then? (We know. You'll be happy to take his phone call at any time.)

As you get older, you'll realize that you're going to die and will be forced to take one of two positions: that your entire life and the lives of your family and children meant nothing—or that they were special. Were you just an accident? If that's true, you are not much different than a horse or a cat. When you die, you will be buried like other animals and that will be the end of it. Talk about striking out with the bases loaded!

Maybe, it will be the church that helps you to see that humans are special. Religious people can't prove everything they believe, but they *hope* there is much more to life than just being a nice animal. Maybe you will too, if you give it a chance. Go to church once a month for six months or go every week for a while, and see what happens. You can always go back to living like a very nice and very smart animal, without any hope for a future life.

Can nice animals go to church just to please their spouse and kids—even if they don't believe right now? We think so. The authors attended a church that had a "sinners Mass." It was at 6:00 P.M. on Sundays, after most of the pro football games were over. We're all sinners, so maybe you can find a Mass like that on a Saturday or Sunday. No one will ever put you down at a Catholic Mass. Our church is a church of big-time sinners and slackers. So go anyway, and feel like you're contributing to your country, your family, and your community.

It's a tradition at many churches to gather after Mass for coffee and donuts. There's the story of parents who bought a doughnut machine for home use. Their five-year-old-son said "That's amazing! Now we don't have to go to church anymore." If you need donuts, let us know and we'll bring you some.[2]

PART TWO

Psychology and Religion.
Who are our Church leaders?
Can they help us now?

Chapter 4

Priests: Who are these men in black? Can our priests hold up against in-depth psychological testing?

This book isn't about the lives of priests, but the authors have conducted psychological evaluations of priesthood applicants for over 35 years. Who are these people? What are they like? Mama's boys who were pressured into the priesthood? The first born male who is fulfilling a parental promise to God? Entrepreneurs, retired businessmen, widowers?

Before the Church sends candidates to psychologists for evaluation, how do these candidates start the discernment process? Many dioceses have used vocation posters geared to men who may have a calling to the priesthood. One such poster reads: "Inquire Within." And the diocese doesn't just mean to inquire within the diocesan offices. Potential seminarians need to look deep within themselves, through prayer and a personal look at their psychological makeup and goals. It's not a vocation to be taken lightly, nor an easy life to live. A more appropriate announcement for vocations to the priesthood might look something like this:

"Wanted: Men In Black looking for low-paying job with strict uniform requirements, sworn obedience to their boss, long hours, 24/7 on call, no marriage or children permitted, and responsibility for the souls of thousands of people. Job skills require an aptitude for teaching, preaching, accounting, counseling, property management, and fundraising. Personal qualities must include intelligence, verbal skills, social skills, patience, self-control, and the ability to relate to all kinds of people, including the sick and dying—and the mother of the bride. All applicants will receive extensive psychological evaluations (because you would have to be crazy to want this job)."

These admission standards rule out mama's boys who were forced into the priesthood and the first born male who is fulfilling a parental promise. They certainly rule out anyone who is looking to "escape from the real world." But they don't rule out entrepreneurs, retired businessmen, widowers, students, and or members of the working class.

They don't even rule out men who are married or who have children. Some married men began as Episcopal priests and then converted to Catholicism and the Catholic priesthood. And married men can become Greek Orthodox priests. The Orthodox Catholic Church broke off from the Roman Catholic Church in 1054, but is a close neighbor—or maybe a cousin.

The authors have found that priests come from a wide range of backgrounds and that they are both ordinary and exceptional at the same time. The seminarian biographies on the webpage of one diocese introduce us to: a former Methodist seminarian, a legislative assistant, an aerospace engineer, a youth minister, a missionary, a mechanical engineer, a musician, a marketing graduate, an animal trainer, a firefighter, an historian, a soldier, a recent high school graduate, an accountant, an entrepreneur, a teacher, a judge, a technology director, a cook, and a customer services specialist.

Not a professional fisherman in the bunch! They come from Florida, New York, Illinois, Pennsylvania, Virginia, Tennessee, Cameroon, Puerto Rico, Colombia, Poland, India, Vietnam and the Philippines.

These fine men have a wide range of personalities that are evident during interview and testing. While they demonstrate intellectual and academic abilities, strong values, good self-control, respect for authority, and the ability to relate to and care for others, there is no single "personality type." They tend to display a sense of humor and a genuine interest in serving others. But their fashion sense, interests, and hobbies vary greatly. Some enjoy a good cigar and classical music. Others relax by working out and listening to pop music.

We find a range of personality dimensions as well. One of the measures used in their psychological evaluations is the 16PF (16 Personality Factor Questionnaire)[1], which provides scores on each of 16 personality dimensions. While most seminarians tend to place fairly high on factors of emotional stability, rule-following, reasoning, and trust, they differ on many of the other dimensions. They may be socially bold or reserved, lively or serious, sensitive or utilitarian, traditional or open to change, group-oriented or self-reliant.

We authors are not claiming we have given these assessments for eons, but when we gave John the Baptist the 16PF, we were a little surprised by the results (Initials are placed between the two extremes of a trait. The extreme traits are highlighted when the person's personality closely matches one of the extremes.):

Reserved	. . **JB**	Warm
Concrete	. . . . . . **JB**	**Abstract**
Reactive	**JB**	Emotionally Stable
Deferential	. . . . . **JB** .	**Dominant**
Serious	. **JB**	Fun-loving
Expedient	. . . . . **JB** .	**Rule-Conscious**
Shy	. . . . . . **JB**	**Socially bold**
Tough	**JB**	Sensitive
Trusting	. . . . . **JB** .	**Vigilant**
Grounded	. . . . . . **JB**	**Abstracted**
Forthright	**JB**	Private
Self-Assured	**JB**	Apprehensive
Traditional	. . . . . . **JB**	**Open to change**
Group-Oriented	. . . . . **JB** .	**Self-Reliant**
Disorderly	**JB**	Perfectionistic
Relaxed	. . . . . . **JB**	**Tense**

We were struck by the number of extreme personality traits that John the Baptist demonstrated. He certainly was not a man with moderate tendencies or a well-balanced personality.

A very different profile emerged when the authors administered the 16PF to Simon Peter:

Reserved	. . . . **SP** . .	Warm
Concrete	. **SP**	Abstract
Reactive	. . . **SP** . . .	Emotionally Stable
Deferential	. . . **SP** . . .	Dominant
Serious	. **SP**	Fun-loving
Expedient	. . . . . **SP** .	**Rule-Conscious**
Shy	. . **SP**	Socially bold
Tough	. **SP**	Sensitive

Trusting		.	.	SP	.	.	.	.	Vigilant
Grounded	SP	.	.	.	.	.	.		Abstracted
Forthright		.	.	SP	.	.	.	.	Private
Self-Assured		.	.	.	SP	.	.	.	Apprehensive
Traditional		.	SP	.	.	.	.	.	Open to change
Group-Oriented	.	.	SP	.	.	.	.		Self-Reliant
Disorderly		.	.	.	.	SP	.	.	Perfectionistic
Relaxed		.	.	.	SP	.	.	.	Tense

We found Peter to be a much more balanced person, with a tendency to be grounded, practical, and perhaps even a little concrete in his thinking. Peter certainly appeared to be more suited for the priesthood than did John the Baptist, who seemed better suited to be a voice shouting in the wilderness.

We're not entirely sure what psychological criteria Jesus used in choosing his apostles, but despite his lack of a license in clinical psychology and a doctoral degree from an APA (American Psychological Association) accredited university, the authors will stipulate that Jesus was pretty good at evaluating people. But, of course, he had one major advantage over other psychologists. He created who he wanted—so he knew them from the beginning.

Our assessment of that Judas fellow showed him to be extremely expedient and reactive, but that's a story for another time.

Our admiration for priests is obvious and we count some of them as personal friends as well. This can be a lonely calling and people in the pews do what they can to support their priests, socially and emotionally. During the Mass we pray for our military and first responders. Priests need to be included in these prayers of the faithful because they are as much first responders as the military, police, or firefighters.

These devout and divinely inspired priests, along with ministers, rabbis, imams, and many other religious leaders, hold a critical position in the defense of spirituality and the defense of our civilization.

Chapter 5

Should we listen to a priest or a psychologist?

When we have significant problems in living, should we pray to God or consult a psychologist or other mental health specialist? This reminds us of the story of a devout woman who was in a sinking boat. She prayed to God for help, but the boat kept sinking. A helicopter happened to come by and the pilot offered to help her. "No, she said, God will take care of me." A while later, a Coast Guard cutter came by, but she refused help. A third rescuer was also turned away. Finally, the boat sank and she drowned.

When she got to heaven she was a little put out and asked St. Peter why God didn't save her. St. Peter said, "We sent you three rescuers, and you turned them all down. Were you expecting a fleet of angels?" Yes, God moves in mysterious ways, and he also gives us free will to make choices.

If you're fortunate, you will have input from priests as well as psychologists, physicians, and other trained professionals. If you're a Catholic, you have the opportunity to meet with a priest during confession. Some priests have a real knack of helping folks with problems in this world, but they often don't have time to spare and they don't have the training that a Catholic psychologist has.

While most people don't avail themselves of psychological services, they really should. Psychologists, counselors, social-workers, psychiatric nurses, and psychiatrists can help with problems that we all share. They use scientific research to help folks know themselves better and cope with minor and major difficulties. If you can change some life-long negative habits, it can also make you more receptive to God's graces.

Unfortunately, some practitioners don't consider our religious values and beliefs when making recommendations. We believe the soul needs nourishment as well as the mind and body. Your priest or bishop may have a list of practitioners for you to contact.

Chapter 6

Happier in this world? Do Church teachings help us to lead happier and more successful lives right here in the pews?

Our Church's primary focus is love of God and hope for an eternity with God. While social issues are important, our primary focus is on God. As Jesus said, "The poor will always be with us."

This Catholic emphasis on our future life separates us from some American Christians. As Ross Douthat points out, popular American theology has included Joel Osteen, Mary Baker Eddy, and the Church of Scientology. Osteen became almost as popular as Billy Graham, but his message was certainly unlike that of Graham. "His (Osteen's) God, gives without demanding, forgives without threatening to judge, and hands out His rewards in this life rather than in the next." Mary Baker Eddy emphasized prayer-driven healing. According to Douthat, L. Ron Hubbard's Scientology also followed the pray and grow rich philosophy.[1]

While we push for hope in the after-life, we Catholics can also benefit during our earthly existence. Here are a few things we psychologists-in-he-pews have noticed.

1. Confession (Sacrament of Penance and Reconciliation), is a really good place to start. As professional counselors, we recognize the value of self-disclosure. Dr. Sidney M. Jourard at the University of Florida conducted extensive research on self-disclosure and its mental-health benefits. Generally speaking, the more open people are about revealing their inner selves, the healthier they are. Jourard believed this included counselors as well as their clients.[2]

Of course, the main benefit of Confession is the sincere desire and resolution to change one's life with the help of God's grace. But the psychological benefits of confession are also well-established.[3] People pay good money to psychologists to reveal what's on their minds. Confession is a safe place to disclose the private, inner self, and Catholics get it for free. And they don't have to wait several weeks to get an appointment! Yes, Confession is a place to "spill the beans" with an open-heart. Don't expect psychoanalysis, but this is definitely a church institution that can help one live a better and happier life here in this world.

2. Free will. The Church believes God created man as a thinking being, a person who can initiate and control his own actions.[4] Our experience with patients young and old makes it clear that lack of control is a significant cause of anxiety.

Too much self-centeredness leads to narcissism (self-admiring at the expense of others), which is one of the most prevalent of mental disorders. Freedom is essential for mental health, but the Church makes it clear that we are not fully self-sufficient. There must be a healthy balance.

The dangers of pride go to back to the Old Testament, beginning with the story of Adam and Eve. Popular mythology also recognizes the problem of exaggerated pride (hubris) in its many stories of legendary heroes. We're all tempted to believe that we can do it all, and on our own, or at least take most of the credit for successful outcomes. Frank Sinatra's great recording of "My Way" is a good example of the temptation to take sole credit for a positive outcome.

We Americans love to think we're independent and don't rely on others, but it's interesting to note that the typical adult in the United States lives only 18 miles from his or her mother.[5]

3. The Church teaches that the family is the original cell of social life. Authority and stability come from the family and are the foundations for freedom and security within society. The fourth commandment reminds children to honor their father and mother.

As psychological practitioners, we have seen individuals who were rejected or abused by their parents, and it would be dishonest for these patients to say they truly loved and respected their parents. But even in those cases, children, as adults, can respect the institution of the family. We believe they still have some responsibility to their parents. That's how important the family is.

There are hundreds of research articles showing the importance of the family in producing happy and successful adults. Children and families with a father and mother do much better in school and in the workplace than children without both parents. One of the reasons for this is that it takes two parents to teach children self-control.

It's ironic, because we used to call this nagging. We can remember when nuns were criticized for nagging their students, but it's interesting to note how well those students did in school and in their careers. Self-control, along with motivation, academic ability, and concentration, are necessary ingredients for college work as well as successful technical and career education.

4. The church has always emphasized charitable giving. Most people don't realize that the Catholic Church is the largest charitable organization in the world.[6] This includes the Red Cross, the Salvation Army, and other marvelous institutions. In the early days of the papacy, it was the pope (the Bishop of Rome) who instituted the first care for homeless people. This is continued today with Catholic Charities and other Catholic ministries.

If you look at the Forbes charity list and select all of the Catholic organizations, the amount is astounding! Adding up just Catholic Charities, Food for the Poor, Catholic Relief Services, St. Jude's, and America's Second Harvest totals $5,570,000,000. Continuing down the list you find Father Flanagan's Homes, Catholic Medical Mission Board, Covenant House, and more.

Add the thousands of other Catholic charities, from Missionaries to the Poor, Amigos for Christ, soup kitchens, homeless shelters, religious orders (such as Missionaries of Charity), along with thousands upon thousands of individual parishes across the globe that often do their work in anonymity, and you will see some of the charitable works of the Catholic Church.[7]

And charity doesn't mean just giving money to poor people. It means a charitable attitude in dealing with others. It means resisting criticism, verbal bullying, and elitism. Nothing is more rewarding than giving of ourselves and nothing contributes more to our mental health. Most of our clients and patients have found that volunteering does them more good than the people they're volunteering to help. One cannot get—without giving.

5. Respect for authority. Catholics are often criticized for their allegiance to the pope and other Church authorities. The authors have had people confront them with the charge that the Catholic Church is not democratic—a clear hint that our Church is un-American. They are right about the Church not being democratic.

We don't remember Christ taking a vote of the apostles before undertaking a miraculous event. We believe in a line of succession from Christ to St. Peter and down to our popes and bishops. This does not mean authorities do not make mistakes or cannot be sinful. Remember, we are a Church of sinners, but this apostolic succession is essential to the Catholic community and its mission.

"The pope represents an institution that matters, whether or not one is a religious believer. The succession of popes, all 262 of them, is the world's oldest dynasty. They touch the consciences, or at least the opinions, of almost a fifth of the human race. The papacy has endured and flourished under emperors, kings and robber barons, under colonial occupations, and confrontation with dictators. And by hook or by crook, it has survived them all."[8]

We must accept legitimate authority. The authors are reminded of the campus rioting during the Vietnam War when the president of the University of Notre Dame, the late Father Theodore Hesburgh, instituted the "15-minute rule." Protesting students had to cease their unlawful activities or turn in their student I.D. cards and leave the university. They were given 15 minutes to comply. This firm order helped both students and faculty, and is still remembered today. Too bad other authority figures didn't have the guts to stand up to well-meaning but naïve and irresponsible young people.

We've seen plenty of families in our private practice and often the children are looking for more structure. They feel unsafe and anxious when they don't know what the rules are. As a result, we give parents charts that cover bedtimes, allowances, and study times, to help provide structure.

We admire the required daily public prayer found in the Muslim Faith. The Catholic Church also provides structure when it expects the faithful to attend services on Sunday and Holy Days and to make a sacrifice during Lent, such as abstaining from meat (even in places like Florida where the seafood is much better than the meat)!

6. The common good. The church teaches that the common good requires respect for the person. As mentioned earlier, our parishes are made up of people from various social classes. No one is less discriminatory than the Catholic Church. One of the authors worked with Carl Rogers, a famous psychologist who was the first mental health researcher to measure the benefits of counseling. He believed in unconditional, positive regard.[8b]

One time Rogers worked with a mentally ill patient who was hearing voices and unable to speak. Rogers sat with this man for 20 to 30 hours without speaking and reflected his own feelings of empathy through his expression and patience. Finally, a single tear coursed down the cheek of the patient, and he was able to speak and disclose his inner feelings.

7. Love one another. Basic trust is essential to mental health. It's much better to trust people and to occasionally be taken advantage of than to stay in a protective shell, or to accept the analogy of human relationships as two ships passing in the night. We prefer the concept of two ships passing at twilight and sometimes scraping hulls. When Jesus said love one another, he meant to love unconditionally—including all those folks who have hurt us.

So we try to forgive others and not carry grudges. We often associate love with strong emotional feelings for someone we like or someone, such as a family member who has supported us. But Dr. Rogers, referenced above, insisted on unconditional positive regard for all, and he was influenced by his religious counseling background.

8. Respect for human life. The Catholic Church believes that man is created in the image and likeness of God. Man comes before all other creatures, even before the environment. We all have a duty to preserve the beauty of nature that God has given us, but we are called to remember that man comes first.

We love our pets, but they are not humans. Will we see them in heaven? No one knows. Animals can be important in helping us overcome loneliness and they are often used therapeutically. We authors established a horseback riding program to help handicapped children at two of our special schools.

As Catholics, we don't support abortion and that's because it represents a slippery slope. We know the fetus is alive and human. Supporters of abortion claim the fetus is not human, but it seems to us that this is the same line of reasoning used by the Nazis in Germany where Jews, homosexuals, and Gypsies were defined by the Nazi government as alive, but not human. As a result, there was no reason not to kill them.

According to The World Health Organization (WHO), there are 45 million abortions world-wide, annually. A 2015 report counts all the girls who were never born in China and Korea because of selective abortion and infanticide. Because of this *secular* policy, there are "upwards of 100 million women missing on the Asian Continent today."[9]

Someday, we're hoping science will come to the rescue. When it can be showed that these innocents are able to learn through conditioning or other teaching methods very early in their life in the womb, public opinion will put a stop to abortion. While terminating life is significant spiritually, there are also practical results. Abortion can lead to guilt and depression, sometimes long after the event.

One of the great advantages of our Church is that it has not given in to pressure from changing national or world cultural patterns or well-meaning attempts to give individuals more freedom and opportunity at the expense of life, hope, and our spiritual progress.

9. There are plenty of false gods around, especially in our secular society: fame, power, alcohol, drugs, sex, and lots of other "gods." Research demonstrates the folly of ungodly and hedonistic lifestyles, but we don't need science or the Catholic Church to tell us this. We can simply look at the news and learn about the horrendous outcomes experienced by people who are chasing these false gods—especially when they're worshiping themselves! How fast they go up—but how quickly they come down.

10. We believe Christianity has actually helped America vitalize its economy and private enterprise. Harvard professor Niall Ferguson quoted a member of The Chinese Academy of Social Sciences: "the heart of your culture is your religion: Christianity. That is why the West has been so powerful. The Christian moral foundation of social and cultural life was what made possible the emergence of capitalism and then the successful transition to democratic politics. We don't have any doubts about this."[10]

So there we have it, another picture from the pews: Ten powerful ways Church teachings help us lead happier more successful lives now, in this world.

Chapter 7

The Catholic Church Sex Abuse Crisis: Straight Talk

This is a fictitious conversation between the authors of this book (Authors) and Marie (Marie), a waitress at a local restaurant, who represents some of the people "in the pews" we talk to from time to time. After we shared some tea, Marie had a few questions:

(Marie): What's really going on with this sex abuse thing with priests and kids?

(Authors): We believe that a small number of priests, maybe 2% of all priests, have been guilty of this behavior and they need to be punished, just as any criminal is punished.

(Marie): Does therapy help these people?

(Authors): If they feel guilty and are depressed about their behavior, it could help them, just as it might help any criminal who wants to change, but we've found that most people who are ordered to undergo therapy don't do well. That's because they don't feel a deep need to change, or maybe feel no need to change at all.

(Marie): If the numbers of abusers is that low, what's all the fuss? Aren't there always going to be a few disturbed people in any group?

(Authors): It's true that most of the abuse complaints are over 30 years old and the majority of alleged abusers are dead, but it's normal to hold priests to a higher standard because they have dedicated their lives to God. Most abuse takes place in homes, schools, and other places, but we expect only the highest standard from priests. There are also some people who want to see the Church damaged. Pope Francis believes that some accusations are the work of the Devil. He believes the Church is being persecuted by people who are exaggerating the problem.

(Marie): What's your take?

(Authors): Any parent who has had one of their children sexually assaulted is going to be outraged. And they should be. We do think that some accusations are false or based on hysteria. (We cover hysteria and witch-hunts in PART FIVE of this book.) According to Catholic League President, Bill Donohue, a former Pennsylvania Attorney General who singled out the Catholic Church was recently convicted of perjury and obstruction of justice and was sentenced to prison.

(Marie): Why would someone make this up?

(Authors): Money is one reason. The Church owns property and raises large sums for charity. Lawsuits for money can be a big motivator for both individuals and their attorneys. Another is the sincere belief of some atheists that religion is bad.

(Marie): Shouldn't the bishops just throw these people out of the church?

(Authors): If they're proven guilty in court, then by all means get them out. That won't stop the abuse, though. Most abuse takes place in families, and these sexual predators will just marry, or find jobs where children are left unprotected.

One of the big complaints was that American Bishops covered up these abusers or just sent them on to another parish. Bishops might have feared scandal that would hurt the Church and keep others from church membership, but the chances of bishops routinely and deliberately hiding sexual psychopaths so that they could prey on more victims, is near zero in our opinion. In the 1970's, mental health professionals recommended therapy and a new environment in order to help abusers.

(Marie): I heard that most of these accused priests are homo-sexuals?

(Authors): It appears that a high percentage of the accused clerics were Gay and there is some concern about Gay sexual networks within the Church.

(Marie): Maybe we should just keep homosexuals out of the Church.

(Authors): Remember, Gay priests who have been accused make up less than 2% of priests in the United States, and the Church is open to Gay priests and Gays in the pews.

(Marie): Can't the pope handle this thing?

(Authors): The pope has been accused of dragging his feet. Pope Francis wants us to pray for all victims and has condemned these atrocities with sorrow and shame, but held off on a world-wide summit in Rome for three months until we had more information.

For a scandal that has been brewing for over ten years, we think this is a reasonable plan, despite the frustration of American Bishops.

Our bishops need to stay unified with Rome. The Church has tolerated scandal for many centuries, and with the intervention of the Holy Spirit it has remained dynamic and holy. We predict the same outcome this time—and pray for it.

PART THREE

Can Modern Science *Prove* that Church Origins Were Inspired?

Chapter 8

Taylor Swift and the Camel Riders' Union of Northern Galilee

Sometimes religion seems outdated and even boring (very boring, in fact) when compared to modern day science and technology. It's a lot more fun to use SnapChat, text a friend, or fire off an interesting e-mail, than to study 2000-year-old religious ideas, even if those inspired writings help us lead better lives and grow closer to God. The media, along with friends and teachers, remind us that science is cool. Science is where it's really at—and they are right!

Yes, science is wonderful, but there's no reason to make science the enemy of religion. Despite some occasional bumping and shoving from both sides, the Christian religion actually paved the way for scientific progress and priests and other religious folks have done outstanding scientific work. Science is a friend of religion when scientific methods help us to better understand our faith. And the study of science doesn't have to be boring. Take Taylor Swift, for example.

What are the odds of Taylor Swift, who came from a little town in Pennsylvania, becoming a superstar with millions of fans? What are the odds of that happening by chance? 100 to 1, 1000 to 1 or maybe even 30,000 to 1? When the odds of her success become very high, we know that Taylor Swift and her crew, along with her loyal fans and marketing wizards, had a lot to do with her success. Swift has special talents and an exemplary support system. It isn't just luck. Of course not.

What are the odds that Elvis is still alive? Yes, Elvis keeps showing up (are those shoes still blue?). In the spring of 2016, bettors in London had a choice: they could bet that Elvis Presley would surface in good health, a 2000 to 1 shot, or wager that the Leicester football team would win the English Premier League Championship. Odds? 5000 to 1. But we question whether the odds should have been that high. Apparently, Leicester had shrewdly invested in undervalued players, and bookmaking odds are often determined by the bettors themselves—not exactly a scientific study of probability.[1] (P.S. Leicester won it all!)

How about the lottery? What would you do with $415 million dollars? Buy a few mansions? Get a decent haircut? All of this money was free and available to anyone in the state of Iowa in July, 2016. The only catch was that you had to pick a few correct numbers from a lottery and the probability of your choosing the right numbers was one in 259 million.[2] Hmm, kind of long odds, wouldn't you say? What were the odds for the creation and growth of Christianity?

How Does Science Use Probability?

Scientists use probability all the time. They rely on it. If there is only one chance in 100 that a new medicine is not responsible for the positive changes found with its use, we'll accept the new medicine. After all, 99 out of 100 is pretty good odds. That's how science works; that's how science makes astonishing progress every day. In their graduate training and research, the authors determined the likelihood that a particular behavior was statistically meaningful based upon the probability of that behavior happening by chance.

The end result of all that training is that probability is used in psychological and neuropsychological research and also in sizing up people. Clinical judgment and assessments are based upon statistics and probability. Given available information, the psychologist must use probability to make the proper assessment, diagnosis, and treatment recommendations.

Similar to the authors' task of determining the statistical significance of Christianity, the clinical psychologist must routinely answer the following question: How probable is a particular condition given this particular set of available information?

Jesus Christ is often dismissed because he lived long ago and some folks think, without really thinking, that maybe he was a prophet or a well-meaning fanatic who just got lucky. This assumption presents a monumental problem because it slams the door on faith in Jesus and his church. It would help if secular science could give us some answers. Was Jesus just lucky?

Can we use these scientific probability methods to study Christianity? If the chances of Christianity being some kind of fluke, or myth, is only one in 100, we know it has some special meaning— from a strictly scientific point of view. The Dead Sea Scrolls reveal that prophets tried to make predictions some 300 years before the birth of Christ, but today we rely on science.[3]

And the use of probability isn't restricted to the fields of psychology and medicine. Not at all. Even in the rarefied air of quantum mechanics we find scientists turning to probability. The field of quantum mechanics shows that no object has a definite position except when colliding with something else (tough way to make a living!).

These leaps in space don't occur in a predictable way, but rather at random. It's just not possible to predict where an electron will appear. So what do scientists do? They calculate the probability that the object will pop up here or there. The question of probability goes to the heart of physics today because quantum mechanics have replaced the entire mechanics of Newton.[4]

Sometimes scientists demand incredibly high odds before certifying a new finding. This is especially true when studying something as enormous as outer space. Recently, a tiny blip from the Hadron Collider in Switzerland predicted a new particle in space that might have connections to dark matter in the universe. If true, this would be an astonishing finding.

The blip scientists found in the data would ordinarily be accepted if the probability reached the level of not one in 100, but one in 10,000. When investigating the impenetrable area of outer space, scientists decided to raise the bar to one in 3.5 million! Even though scientists had never seen, smelled, or touched the particle, if that level of probability was reached, scientists would claim the new particle actually existed and was not a fluke.[5]

On the face of it, most people would think such demands are unrealistic, but scientific findings are often not logical. Rather, they are sometimes counter-intuitive (against reason) and proof of reliability and validity must be precise, especially in previously unexplored areas.

What is probability? Some things are possible but not probable, such as an American living on Mars only five years from now. Some things are impossible, such as a grown elephant living inside a standard-sized thimble, or highly unlikely, such as Donald Trump and Bill Clinton joining forces to found a monastery for cloistered monks. Many things are probable—they will probably happen. What are the odds of winning the videogame Batman: Arkham Knight on the first try? Kind of low, we suspect.

Have you ever wondered about the odds of playing men's college basketball? Shouldn't be too hard if you're willing to shoot 100 free throws every day. Right? There are 347 Division I college basketball teams. Each team offers 13 scholarships. Hence, there were about 4,511 Division I college basketball players in 2016. How does this compare with the pool of young men that could potentially play?

One and one-half million young men graduate from high school each year. Since anyone who graduated over the past 4 years could play on a current college team, this gives us a pool of 6 million young men who could potentially play men's college basketball. With 4,511 rosters spots from a pool of 6 million, there is a 1 in 1,330 chance that a typical male high school graduate will play college basketball.[6] (We haven't forgotten women players—a close relative of the authors played on the first women's basketball team at the University of Notre Dame—mighty tough odds for her, as well!)[7]

Can't I Have Faith Without Science?

Of course, some folks who are already religious and have a strong faith may not need or even desire scientific input. They don't want to be "Doubting Thomases" like the Apostle Thomas. Biblical writings indicate that he had to feel Jesus' wounds before he would believe.

"Thomas (who was called Didymus, the twin), one of the twelve, was not with the other apostles when Jesus visited them. So the other disciples told him, 'We have seen the Lord.' But he said to them, 'Unless I see the mark of the nails in his hands, and put my finger in the mark of the nails and my hand in his side, I will not believe."

According to these Gospels, a week later the disciples were again in the house where Jesus had visited them and Thomas was with them. Although the doors were shut, Jesus came and stood among them and said, "Peace be with you." Then he said to Thomas, "Put your finger here and see my hands. Reach out your hand and put it in my side. Do not doubt, but believe."

Thomas answered him, "My Lord and my God!" Jesus said to him, "Have you believed because you have seen me? Blessed are those who have not seen and yet have come to believe."

Yes, you are truly blessed if you believe without proof, but science doesn't draw conclusions based on faith—nor should it. There's a lot more to learning and understanding than just science, but science makes progress based on probability and statistical proof. It's normal for Christians to have doubts or difficulties with their faith from time to time, so it helps to know that science and religion can work together. This is the reason the authors are examining the birth of Christianity from a strictly scientific point of view in this book.

What Does Probability Tell Us About Christianity?

How did we do this? First, we only accepted facts related to the life of Christ. Facts based on the writings of secular and Jewish historians living and writing at that time; not the writings of Christ's followers which are found in the Bible and Church tradition. We measured the dynamic spark of Christianity from those bare-boned, non-religious facts, alone.

Granted, strong and convincing arguments for a belief in Christianity can be made through the study of the times in which Christ lived, along with Old Testament prophecies and the gospels of the New Testament. Yes, the power of reason alone convinces many folks that Jesus was the Messiah. But this is not compelling evidence for scientists. Science demands more than just reason, and reason, all by its lonesome, doesn't seem to get atheists or agnostics all tingly either, we might add.

For example, scientists might question Christ's extraordinary proclamations in the Temple, as a child. Even if they agreed that this could have happened, they might wonder if Jesus was the secret pupil of a brilliant Old Testament scholar and had the equivalent of a Ph.D.? Remember the old TV show, Dragnet? Today, scientists emulate Joe Friday when they say, "Just the facts, Ma'am, just the facts."

Some scientists do believe in a higher power in their own personal lives, based on reason, but they must have proof, not centuries of study and wisdom, when they practice their profession. In their jobs, they are required to operate within accepted scientific boundaries.

What did our scientific investigation reveal? We found that the idea of Christianity just being a myth that someone invented is remarkably improbable, from a strictly scientific point of view. In fact, the odds of Christianity being a concocted myth, written many years later, are not just one in 100 or even one in 3 million, but rather one in 10+ million. (We are saving the exact figure for later, to encourage you, the reader, to stick with us to the pitiless mathematical end).

Just picture 10+ million one-inch boxes spread out over several football fields. A drone flies over the football fields and releases a single penny. One of the little boxes is marked, and the chance, or probability, of that penny falling into that marked box is one in 10+ million. Wow! Not exactly likely, would you say? And scientists would agree with you.

Scientific probability makes it clear that if you fly that drone over the tiny boxes again, it does not reduce the chances of the penny falling into the correct box—to one in 5+ million and then with a third flight to one in 2½+ million—no, the odds remain the same each time: one in 10+ million. Yes, our research shows Christianity to be a statistically unique occurrence. A miraculous event? Scientists don't use terms such as miracle unless they're talking about a successful "Hail Mary" pass in a Green Bay Packers vs. Dallas Cowboys playoff game or the Chicago Cubs world series championship.

Let's compare our finding with the probability of your old high school winning the state championship in soccer. If your school is playing against teams with a similar skill level and there are 60 potential state-wide opponents, your chances of winning it all are 1 in 60. Not great odds, but that's nothing compared to the chances of the Christian Church's incredible winning ways against the mighty Roman Empire.

And, unlike a high school soccer team, the Christian church, if we can believe anything the Bible says, as well as non-Christian historians of the time, didn't start with players who had lots of practice over many years. Nope, just the equivalent of a bunch of ninth grade volunteers (the apostles) who had only a brief time to learn and practice—before spreading the word about Christianity.

Actually, the odds of 1 in 60 means it's even pretty rare to win the state soccer championship. When did your high school last win it—or did your school ever win state? Think of that drone flying overhead, a penny, and 60 little boxes down there in one corner of the end zone. And then think of 10+ million little boxes.

Here are some other comparisons: What were the odds of:

Donald Trump winning the Republican presidential nomination? Oh my, the Donald.

You and your family and friends getting along 100% of the time. We know, your big brother always starts it!

The survival and growth of the American Colonies. That British Navy was one huge mother. If you don't believe us, ask big George (King of bloody England).

Creating the McDonald's franchise to sell Big Macs. Lots of special sauce, but the French fries made it worthwhile.

Adolf Hitler initiating the Nazi Party which led to World War II?

Yep, there are lots of things we would like to know and predict, and scientific probability studies are relied upon by all scientists to give us greater mathematical precision. So where do we go from here?

Chapter 9

Scientific research is a cool detective story. Sherlock?

Some people hear the terms *scientific* and *method,* and anticipate boredom. We think otherwise. We believe the reader will find this chapter to be interesting and revealing.

There are at least three commonly used research methods: Most psychological studies set up an artificial situation where all variables (things that can influence the research in any way) can be tightly controlled. We will see this with Dr. Baumeister's study of self-control later in this chapter.

A second uses physical material and observation to analyze evidence from the past. The many studies of the Shroud of Turin are a good example of this approach, and it is reviewed in greater detail in Appendix II. A third approach relies almost entirely on probability, and that's the one we'll be following, but, as you will soon see, we've added an important wrinkle.

Modern neuropsychologists have probed the brain using MRIs and other scans. United States President Barack Obama compared brain mapping to "the space race of the 1960s." But most people don't realize that modern neuroscientists continue to look to outside behavior in the real world to verify their findings. Dr. Kristan Kennedy's research at The Center for Vital Longevity at the University of Texas in Dallas shows how little we know about the brain and its 100,000,000,000 neurons.[1] Yes, that's 100 billion of these little connectors and message carriers!

So how can scientific methods open the door to the birth of Christianity and its influence over the past 2000 years? We propose to follow in the footsteps of psychologists who objected to simply using logic and reasoning to understand people. When the authors of this book were in training, such reliance on logic—think Sigmund Freud—was referred to as "armchair speculation."

B.F. Skinner was highly successful in his study of human behavior.[2] If you reward an animal or a person soon after they do something, they will be inclined to repeat the behavior. Today, whenever a parent rewards a child's good behavior with a treat or sends a child to timeout for misbehavior, they are following Skinner's methods. Other areas of application include education, business, advertising, the military and all areas of life involving motivation and reward.

An interesting example is the use of these techniques by nuns in America's classrooms. This is a brief digression for fun and for nun-lovers like us. While popular stories had the nuns using rulers to smack errant fingers, they were highly sophisticated in their use of Pavlov's classical conditioning and Skinner's operant conditioning.

For example, they often sat behind their students during Mass and used a "clicker" to remind students to stop whispering and settle down. The clicker became associated with a negative outcome the kids had received from the nuns previously when they misbehaved. Something like Pavlov's dogs associating the ringing of a bell with food (classical conditioning). No, we're not saying Catholic students were "dogged" in their irreverent behavior (more corny jokes to come!).

Another use was the awarding of Holy Cards with pictures of saints in heaven for good behavior (operant conditioning). We psychologists kid the nuns about this one, because the reward should come soon after a behavior in order to reinforce it and change it. Waiting until heaven is a bit too long for most 10-year-olds! But getting a Holy Card was a signal that they had done well, and they were happy.

Some people think of psychological research as "soft science," but quite the opposite is true. These critics are confusing "pop psychology" with the hard science that has made psychological research essential to medicine, and yes, the development of neuroscience and magnetic resonance imaging (MRI). As early as 1954, psychologist Paul Meehl said that "algorithms (statistics) beat subjective expert judgment, and they are quicker and cheaper."[3]

In fact, the authors can remember a time when leading physicians were convinced that the brain, like hardening cement, was set in adolescence or early adulthood, allowing no room for change or growth after that time. Meanwhile, at the University of Florida and other institutions, neuropsychologists were establishing evidence for the plasticity (changeability) of the brain. Their findings meant that the brain can change during all stages of one's lifetime (although we admit that some wives think their husbands' brains are permanently anchored at the 16-year-old level).

Getting back to Dr. Skinner's behavior and reward system, how did he do it? He simply gave up on guessing about the inner workings of the mind. While he agreed that the theories of Freud and other great thinkers were interesting and gave useful insight into human motivation, they still lacked scientific rigor. As a result, many of those theories were short-lived or conflicted with other theories. No, science was the way to go.

Skinner's brilliant breakthrough was his "black box" research design. Rather than making sophisticated inferences (guessing) as to how the brain worked, Skinner said let's pretend to put a black box over the brain. We will then observe what goes into the box on one side and what comes out on the other side. That way we can avoid inside-of-the-box reasoning and speculation altogether.

Here's an example of a scientific (black-box) vs. non-scientific approach to understanding human motivation. In research by Roy Baumeister at Florida State University, children were offered a treat if they could wait before eating a nice big helping of chocolate cake placed directly in front of them. Researchers measured which children were able to delay their responses, (what goes into the black box) and then followed the kids' activities and achievements for several years afterwards (what comes out the other side of the box).[4]

What did they find? They found that self-control is very important in motivation and success, and that it starts early. But they did not guess at, or make inferences about, why or how the children managed or did not manage to restrain themselves. In other words, they didn't try to get inside the box (the brain) because they felt it would be more reliable to stay outside of the box. Children's brains are usually not developed, and their answers to questions may not be reliable enough for good long-term research.

If Sigmund Freud had been asked to determine why some kids could delay eating the chocolate cake while other kids couldn't, he might have interviewed them, asking (inside the box of their brains) why they could or couldn't wait for the cake. Freud undoubtedly would have come up with some interesting ideas or speculations as to why the kids differed in self-control, because he was a highly creative genius.

But in the end, Freud wouldn't have known about self-control from a scientific point of view. And he would have had a tough time predicting how all of this influenced the kids' behavior in the future. And, of course, scientific findings don't have to be logical. For example, we might have guessed, based on common sense that more mature appearing kids who had had a big breakfast that day would be more likely to hold off on receiving the reward. But what it they didn't?

Evidence for the specialness of the life of Christ to this point has involved *inside of the box* analyses that relied on the statements of witnesses, or alleged witnesses to his life (New and Old Testament Bibles, church tradition, and the Freud's of our Church, such as St. Augustine and Thomas Aquinas. These folks have provided rich ideas and we're not saying or implying that they were incorrect—or unreliable. But we're after more than common sense.

A Pharisee (Jewish folks "in the pews," not the elite) of the Sanhedrin (local courts and judges) by the name of Gamaliel is *alleged* to have said, in regard to the claims of the Apostles, "My advice is that you have nothing to do with these men. Let them alone. If their purpose or activity is human in its origin, it will destroy itself. If, on the other hand, it comes from God, you will not be able to destroy them without fighting God himself."[5]

Sounds great, doesn't it? But we can't use it in our study because it's clearly inside the box. It's an alleged statement that we can't prove was actually said. No, we're staying outside the box of church tradition and reason, marvelous though it may be.

What we're proposing here is to put a black box over the life of Christ and restrict ourselves to outside-of-the-box-secular facts. What goes into the black box are facts that include the existence of Jesus Christ. How do we know he even existed? He was identified by a major non-Christian historian of the time. We also have unquestioned and reasonable information as to the number of years Jesus lived, the length of his preaching, and the approximate time of his death, also noted by non-Christian historians. What comes out the other side of our black box are facts related to the travels of his followers and the growth of his church.

Self-Control Study

Goes into black box:		Comes out of black box:
Resisting eating cake:		Kids who resisted did better with school, careers & happiness.

Birth of Christianity

Goes into black box:		Comes out of black box:
Factual history of Jesus		Growth and number of followers, birth, death & persecutions longevity & importance

Please don't confuse this black box approach with thinking outside the box, which refers to original or creative thinking. Our black box lets us stick to facts before and after an event in order to avoid non-scientific speculation about what's inside the box.

What can we learn from these bare-boned facts? We can measure with scientific accuracy the probability of a sect that operated within a time frame of only 6 months to 3 years and followers comprised of farmers, fishermen, and other common rural citizens, who claimed their leader was God, lasting for some 2000 years and influencing over 2 billion people.

We will compare these figures with examples of the progress and continuity of other sects, projects, and innovations. If our research shows scientifically significant statistical results, based on this secular evidence alone, it will support the belief that this historical figure and his followers were distinctive and extraordinary.

This data can also be compared to current scientific research and the probability figures used by scientists' day-in-and-day-out that demand our respect. So we are definitely going to take the high road of science, which is sometimes not logical, and not get tangled up with any of that "nasty old reasoning."

Visualize yourself in a sleek and radiant glider floating quietly over a deep blue lake, with the wind fingering your hair. Peer down at the nearby swampland, teeming with wildlife, tangled vines, and murky rivers. Beyond the dirty smog-covered swamp is a congested city with stymied traffic, pollution, and worst of all, gads—people; left-brained people who use logic and reasoning to confuse themselves and others. They're so picky, picky, picky. We're flying over all of that. Great, isn't it?

Chapter 10

Wow! A real wow story. The results give us the proof we had hoped for.

Once we had decided on our research design, we were ready to begin our scientific study of Christianity. How did we conduct this research? First, to satisfy scientific standards, we needed to establish that Christ actually lived. We checked history books from the time of Jesus and found a Jewish aristocrat, politician, and historian, by the name of Joseph ben Matthias. He was commonly known as Flavius Josephus, and he lived from A. D. 37-38 to sometime after the year 100. He wrote two great books: *The Jewish War* and *The Jewish Antiquities.*[1]

In the Jewish Antiquities, Josephus wrote about a meeting of judges and referred to "Jesus-who-is-called Messiah." He also recounted the execution of John the Baptist and noted that Pilate was notorious for his cruelty. The Roman historian Tacitus also recounted Roman Emperor Nero's cruelty to a sect called "Christianos." Finally, a reference is found in the Babylonian Talmud's *Tractate Sanhedrin* (an encyclopedia of Jewish history and culture) which refers to "Yeshu (Jesus) who was hanged on the eve of Passover."[1b]

We are fortunate to have this evidence of Jesus' existence, because Jesus lived in a tiny outpost of the mighty Roman Empire and it comes from non-Christian historians, who lived at the time of Christ.

The above secular facts comprise the front end of our research box—the facts that go into the front of the black box. What comes out the other end of the box? While it is not possible to track the growth of the early church with great precision, most reliable information indicates that by the end of the second century A.D., those who professed Christianity reached 40-60 million.[2]

By the year 300, 10.3% of the world was Christian.[3] Within five centuries, millions of followers spread out from India in the East, Ethiopia in the South, and Britain in the West. So if we just stay with outside of the box facts and don't rely on any church teachings or writings found in the New Testament or church tradition, we know that Jesus really lived, and we know that the early growth of the church was rapid. We also know that today Christianity has 2.5 billion followers.

What are the odds of the Christian church exploding onto the scene, growing so quickly, and lasting for 2000 years? It sounds like the answer is obvious, but first we must deal with objections to mathematical probability (this could be slightly boring, but won't last long). One objection might be the question of randomness, or luck versus skill. The odds of winning the State of Iowa lottery are stupendous but if millions are trying it, someone has to win.

Did Christianity just get lucky? The answer to this randomness question is that millions of people were not trying to establish religions in competition with Jesus, and the outcome for Christianity was far greater than even the hundreds of millions of dollars paid out in a lottery. Also, crucifixion and a dozen skeptical followers are not exactly the same as winning the lottery jackpot in the great state of Iowa!

People do get lucky. A poker player at a casino wins hand after hand until her luck finally runs out. Did Jesus' luck run out? It could have. But there is no historical evidence that Jesus was trying to establish a political entity. There were others at that time wanting to overthrow the Roman occupation, but their names have been lost through time.

We think there was probably nothing political in Jesus' ministry, but from outside of the box we can't know for sure. If he was making plans for a future political entity when he was executed, wouldn't this weaken his base of support and terrify his followers? Isn't the concept behind capital punishment to stop a person and their influence?[4] Martyrs can and do motivate folks—but for 2000 years?

Are there other cautions when it comes to statistical predictions? We must consider what scientists call a ceiling effect. For example, we would expect taller students to do better in basketball, on average, in grade school and high school, because they can get more rebounds and layups are easier. But there are so many tall players in college and professional basketball that the relationship between height and basketball effectiveness starts to break down. All of a sudden, it stops. It's as though there is an invisible ceiling. Scientists call this the ceiling effect.

And with any research we do, we need to get our facts straight. Kevin Durant, an NBA star, listed himself at 6'9" despite actually being 6'11." He justified this fib by saying he wanted to be the perfect size for a small forward. And other players, such as Bill Walton, claimed to be six-foot 11 inches when they were 7 feet tall.[5] So even when we're sure of our facts, we can be mistaken.

Another caution is *regression to the mean*. This research jargon simply means that when you measure a person's performance, you'll want to bet that the next bit of behavior from that person will tend to go back to his or her average overall performance. So people sometimes improve dramatically in some activity or suddenly sink below their average, but the odds are they will go back to their average in the long run, assuming we have enough observations.

Michael Lewis gives the example of Air Force pilots being praised after a great landing and criticized after a terrible one. Officers then noticed that the next landing after a fantastic one was poor while the one after a bad landing was better. Think about your favorite baseball player who is in a batting slump. He'll probably get back to his usual average before too long. When making predictions, we must look at long-term averages and not get too excited about temporary changes.[6]

Are these complexities concerning probability really relevant to our research? Not so much, but they make us proceed carefully. We'd also like to impress you with our research knowledge. You'll be happy to learn that a big flap forced us to accept a little humility. Let's say flapping, because we were taken down a notch by a not very smart bird. A beautiful blackbird. We need to tell you about Nassim Taleb's metaphor of the black swan.

Taleb makes the point that predictions based on probability did not predict the existence of a black swan, but sure enough, someone found one. Taleb describes this as an event so far out of experience we can't even imagine it until it happens.[7] Is Jesus a statistical black Swan? As you will see from our calculations, the probability of predicting Jesus and his religion is greater than Taleb's requirement of

0.0001%. But we view this thinking as support for the special nature of Christianity, rather than as just a criticism of mathematical systems.

Okay, with this bird flap behind us, let's continue with our research. If you're still with us, you've showed good patience and self-control. No chocolate cake for you, but we appreciate your patience.

Ordinarily, predictions that come up with probability quotients such as one in 100 are calculated by merging two factors. The first one is called *anchoring* and it focuses on outside, historical information that could help us in our prediction. For example, let's go back to the Leicester City soccer team. The fact that they had never won a top-tier championship in their 132 years of existence was useful information when coming up with a prediction. This reminds us a little of the Chicago Cubs!

This anchoring factor uses historical information. This is on the outside of our research box and has nothing to do with the second factor, which is inside the box and includes the quality of the young players just recruited for the team, the quality of the competition, playing conditions, scheduling etc.

Here's an example where we have both outside anchoring and inside information: In our opinion, the probability of Donald Trump becoming the Republican nominee for president of the United States based on factor 1, or anchoring, gave him only about a 5 in 100 chance of success. This is because party outsiders have never won the nomination.

Factor 2, current information, gave us a man who had no political or military experience, but who was successful financially and hosted a popular TV show. We know that having success in televised debates has a lot to do with whether "the camera likes you." This man had hundreds of hours in front of TV cameras and was practiced in selling himself.

Marketing is always critical, so despite the fact that Trump faced 16 opponents, including several successful state governors—and his scorched earth remarks during debates mobilized opposition forces—we thought he would do well in a debate format. We gave him a 35% chance based on this inside information (factor 2). Merging these two factors gave him an overall probability of 11.6 in 100. That's still not very high. Don't look now, but sometimes even we get things wrong!

One of our proof readers wasn't satisfied with our claim that Trump had a chance, even though it was a long shot, and wanted us to prove we gave Trump an 11.6 chance before the event. If the prediction was given later, in hindsight, it could influence the results, he thought. This is a very good point, and research does in fact show that hindsight bias is 54%.

The interesting thing here is that this bias is usually applied to people confirming a *winning* prediction that something happened: "I knew that would happen." "I could have predicted that because of this or that factor." It is looking for confirmation or noticing causes in hindsight that we think explain a known outcome.[8]

For Trump, you could say hindsight bias could have increased our reported odds of his nomination. Were we influenced? We can't answer that question, because there is no way for us to go back to a time prior to the debates. The odds of 11.6 in 100 are still not very favorable, however. Imagine that drone flying over a football field with only 11.6 unmarked spaces out of 100, and without looking, dropping a coin into the correct one.

In the case of Jesus, because he lived so long ago, and didn't appear on a popular TV show, we have no scientifically reliable information regarding the second factor, or inside the box information.

Therefore, all of our research on the origins of Christianity is based on factor 1, or anchoring (outside the box calculations). What are those factors?

1. The cultural and sociological conditions out of which the individual or venture evolves (what were the conditions in his neighborhood)? The educational and economic conditions in Nazareth at the time of Jesus are well known to secular historians. Most objective individuals would agree that that these conditions were primitive rather than rich or sophisticated. This means it was very unlikely Jesus benefited from lobbyists, insider dealings, or influential religious or government connections.

According to Christian historian John P. Meier, Jesus was "insufferably ordinary, and his ordinariness included the ordinary status of a layman, without special religious credentials or powerbase." Meier admits that this description may not be accurate. "Jesus wanders in a historical twilight zone in the sense that almost no chronological markers light the path Jesus trod."[9]

John Nagy, associate editor, Notre Dame Magazine, commented on the small family circle, including a handful of shepherds, the night Christ was allegedly born: "No thought leaders these. No key influencers. No masters of first century social media. Just plain country people who slept outside and who, quite literally, smelled of the sheep."[10]

Meier and Nagy give us rich and tempting imagery, but, as with the really cool advice from the Pharisee Gamaliel of the Sanhedrin, these opinions tend to be inside the box. We acknowledge that these are safe inferences based on secular studies of historical sociology and anthropology, but we are going to reject them for our purposes here, because we don't know if these facts accurately tell us how it felt to be on the ground at that time. A cynic might point out that Jesus could have been an exception to his culture and class and was actually born in a five-star Hilton (Another bad joke).

For people at this level to have the business ability and management experience to set up any business is highly doubtful. There's no secular evidence that these guys attended the Wharton School of Finance or got a B.S. in commerce from The Trump School of Real Estate. Setting up fishing tours or selling seafood to the military would be examples of innovative business models, but the chances are 20 to 1 against, and even if established, it's doubtful the project would have lasted more than 20 or 30 years.

Our research shows that most successful religious, political, and business ventures start at a higher socioeconomic and cultural level than did Christianity, and rarely last more than a few years. One study shows that 95% of today's successful entrepreneurs (those who start new businesses), have at least a Bachelor's degree.[11]

Alexandria and Athens had some top-notch universities, but we don't believe the apostles attended them. We're also pretty sure they didn't complete a long-distance learning course titled "Don't Come up Dry: Become a Desert Entrepreneur" offered through the University of Phoenicia. We rate the probability on this factor at about a 1 in 20 chance of success.

2. The amount of time the leader or leaders spend in establishing the venture or enterprise. This may be a weak link in terms of avoiding inside the box information, but we are accepting the estimate of 1 to 3 years. Today, neither secular nor religious historians dispute this time frame. When we compare this amount of time to the history of our planet, it gives clear evidence of the power of this variable. If, as the U.S. Geologic Service reports, our planet is 3.5

billion years old, Christ's ministry of 1 to 3 years is so quick as to be an unmeasurable eye blink.

And what if the starting time was even shorter? What if it really boiled down to the time between the day of Christ's crucifixion and a few days later when he allegedly appeared to his frightened and dispirited followers and sent them on a mission that would lead to certain martyrdom? If true, this makes one think that Christ came to deliver a message and accomplish something very specific. The three years' time in history is truly unique and places the probability of something substantial starting this fast at the 1 in 50 range.

We are saying range, because it's not possible to come up with an exact figure. Why not one in 40 or one in 63? This question emphasizes the limits of any projection based on probability. In many ways, it comes down to common sense (oh, dear) reasoning within an organized scientific framework. How many organizations, businesses or general venture do we know that get off the ground in three years or less?

There have been some, but one in 50 is probably a low ratio. We would rather err on that side than making the odds too great. Our calculations can be found in Appendix 1, *and we invite readers to come up with their own odds in order to compare them with ours.*

3. The amount of organized resistance to the individual, sect, or project, and the quality and degree of resistance—from simple objections to verbal harassment—to physical attacks and murder. David and Goliath? The American Colonies facing the mightiest navy in the history of the world up to that time. Yes, there have been other underdogs who survived overwhelming odds, but Christianity stands right up there with other fragile, powerless, and vulnerable entities. The cruelty of the mighty Roman Empire and its murderous hatred

of prophets at that time is documented by secular historians. The fact that the early Christians survived, again led us to an estimate of 1 in 50.

4. The public relations and media available to promote the new concept or person, including such things as the printing press, books, records, movies, computers, the Internet, telephones, television, Twitter, Facebook, texting, Snapchat, etc. etc. We can't think of anyone, with perhaps the exception of the Old Testament Prophet Abraham, who had an equally poor public relations program (excluding some spiritual presence, of course). The Christians did have word-of-mouth marketing, and this face-to-face approach can be powerful, but it takes time—lots of it. We think there is only a 1 in 30 chance of starting any venture with this level of marketing.

St. Paul wrote visionary letters and Jesus' followers could take slow-moving ships to foreign lands, but these attempts at public relations were almost nonexistent compared to those of Taylor Swift or Hitler's propaganda machine. Swift benefits from some of the most sophisticated public relations ever created. Or take the Continental Army. It at least benefited from printing presses and Benjamin Franklin's visits to France, a potential helper.

5. Number of followers today. For whatever reason, and with no inside the box speculation, Christianity has over two billion followers today. This factor needs no rehashing or interpretation. Not only is this a huge number, especially considering its origins, but it evolved in a continuous fashion, without a break. The authors recognize that there are cultural factors involved in the growth of Christianity, including fertility rates, but this is a number that must be reckoned with.

Since the church was not snuffed out in infancy, there was a reasonable chance that it might grow to include 5000 to 10,000 people. Using this as a basis, it had only a 0.0006 chance of growing as it did. We calculate the odds as one in 1,667.

6. How long it has lasted. Christianity is 2000 years old. What were the odds of lasting so long, back then, in the early days of the church? One in 10,000 is probably conservative.

7. The initial growth spurt, especially the first 50 years, represents a powerful number. As reported earlier, by the end of the second century A.D., those who professed Christianity in the Roman Empire alone numbered 40 to 60 million. By the year 300, 10.3% of the world was Christian.

Does it really matter how fast a venture, philosophy, or concept develops? Yes, it does, because forecasting assumes that history and societies crawl rather than jump. Some might dispute these numbers but no one denies that the growth was incredibly fast.

Nassim Taleb challenged the notion of a gradual crawl when he introduced the black swan concept. The more quickly something explodes or pops, the more we consider it significant. How many new ventures or concepts become a black swan? Let's just sample new businesses in the United States. According to *Forbes Magazine*, there are 28 million small businesses in the United States.[12] In 2004, 580,900 businesses were started and 576,200 closed.[13]

When we extend those figures to every country in the world, we can see that creating a black swan is indeed rare. If viewed as a business, would Christianity have been defined as a small business? Absolutely. We give the Christian initial growth spurt in the first 100 years about one in 10,000.

Research on business startups shows that only one in 500 newly registered businesses in the United States reaches the size of at least

$100 million in revenue. Only one of 17,000 reaches 5 million in revenue and sustains 10 *years* of growth.[14]

But what about Uber, Amazon, and Facebook? Uber's pace of development is amazing, but it started with millions of dollars and a little gizmo called the smartphone—which wasn't real big in Judea 2000 years ago. And the Camel Riders Union would have protested, anyway. Uber, just a few years old, is already meeting stiff competition along with government regulations, and it's changing its business format to driverless cars.

8. The impact of the innovation on an average person's life today. Is it important and significant to many people today? The answer is obvious. It has been highly impactful to billions of people over the centuries, both Christian and non-Christian. Today, the Christian church leads all organizations in charity, with a special focus on the poor and homeless. As we saw previously, Chinese economists are convinced that the Christian moral foundation made the birth of capitalism possible, leading to the successful transition to democratic politics.

It was pretty clear, even at the time of Christ, that anyone who signed up for the "Christ Religion" would be significantly impacted. These folks were truly committed. Probably a 7 in 10 chance of a solid commitment after stirring in some who would quit. Predicting it would still have an impact on an average person's life 2000 years in the future would certainly reduce the probability.

In addition to Christianity's impact on Christians today, we need to factor in its impact on non-Christian lives as well. We could look at the impact of the Ten Commandments on the legal system and western civilization or the widespread cultural impact of the New Testament. Most current readership lists place the Bible in their top ten most influential books. One site (mashable.com) even looked at

Facebook to determine what books were currently in vogue to the point of influencing people's lives, and the Bible placed at number six! At Amazon.com, a recent edition of the Bible received an average of 4.5 stars for its 8,440 reviews.

Perhaps the simplest way to see the impact of the Bible is to look at the number of copies purchased. In the past 50 years, the Bible has sold over 3.9 billion copies. Second place on the list, *Quotations from Mao Tse-tung* sold 820 million copies (Mao was a brutal Chinese dictator who stayed in power for nearly 30 years and who engineered mass starvations that killed millions (the Devil never gives up, does he?).[15] And Harry Potter was third, with 400 million![16]

We are estimating a one in 10,000 chance of such a significant impact in people's lives.

Well, there we have it. In half of the eight calculations, we come up with far less than 1%. And adding all eight of the second numbers, for example 1 in 1000, as found in the first sample, and dividing by eight, we get 1 in 3,977 as our average probability of success for each of the eight conditions.

If all of these probabilities were independent of one another, such as rolling dice multiple times (one roll of the dice does not affect the next roll, thus making their outcomes "independent"), then we would have a simple way to determine the probability of a positive outcome given those eight conditions. We could simply multiply them and would have a total probability of 1 in 2,500,000,000,000,000,000,000. Yes, that is 25 followed by 20 zeros or one in 2.5 sextillion!

But since some of these probabilities are overlapping, such as the size of the following and the significance of its impact, we need to use a more sophisticated method to calculate the probability.

(Trigger warning: for those who have an aversion to mathematics, the following section may cause fatigue, numbness in the toes, coughing spells, the dry heaves, or the popping of skittering brain synapses, urinary tract infection, yeast infection, abnormally low blood pressure, extreme loss of body water, feeling faint, and candida infection of the glands.)

Nate Silver and Stephen Unwin inspired us to consider Bayes' Theorem. Using this approach, we are able to make a more accurate estimate of the probability of an event.[17] Bayes devised a mathematical formula that takes into account an initial estimated probability of an event and then refines the probability each time additional information is available.

Using the initial expectation that starting up a new endeavor would have a one in ten chance of success, and then calculating the refined probability for each of the first four factors above, we find that the chances of finding success are 1 in 187,617, which is a probability of 0.00000533. For a more detailed look at the calculations, please refer to the Appendix l.

Only the first four factors were used in this calculation, because those were the adverse conditions making it unlikely that success would be found. The next four factors look at the exceptional level of success that was reached. Given that success was obtained, we can further estimate that there is still only a 0.0006 chance of having so many followers, a 0.00006 chance of having so many followers and lasting 2000 years, a 0.00003 chance of having so many followers, lasting 2000 years, and having such a rapid initial growth spurt, and a 0.000015 chance of having all of those factors plus a high degree of significance in people's lives.

That is a 1 in 66,667 chance of such a powerful, large, and lasting success, on top of the 1 in 187,617 chance of being successful at all. Putting these figures together, we find the odds of Christianity being so influential with its starting conditions are 1 in 12,507,862,539 (1 in 12.5 billion), which is a chance of 0.00000000008.

At the risk of understatement, the authors believe that even the most conservative and cautious of scientists would find this level of probability to be highly statistically significant!

But what about hindsight bias as discussed as earlier? Hindsight bias may be causing us to search only for examples of causes that would make the outcome less probable. We could be ignoring factors that might make it more probable (such as the psychological need for people to believe in something or to give life meaning, even if the belief is not logical).

We can't go back to the time of Christ and make unbiased predictions about the future of Christianity. All we can do is try to use scientific principles to make a reasonable estimate of probability given what historical evidence is available *outside the box*. However, if we were to ask people who were alive at the time of Christ (or look at what we know about them historically), our guess is that they, too, would have said that establishing a world religion to last over 2,000 years was very unlikely.

Factual information tells us the Jews were looking for a messiah to arrive with an army to defeat Caesar and all enemies. They were very disappointed (and a bit irritated) by the arrival of a carpenter from Nazareth. His own disciples thought the revolution was over when Jesus was crucified. Historians in Rome and around the world made little, if any, mention of Jesus, and he did not make the Forbes list of fastest growing company's top CEOs, or best ideas of the new millennium.

All of this math could be inducing boredom, if not sleep. Is there a simpler and more interesting way to make objective predictions? Another method? We came across a procedure used by sporting enthusiasts to predict the power of a particular athletic team prior to the start of the season (this is more our speed). One of these is a college basketball projection system that comes up with the best offensive coaches.

It evaluates a coach's teambuilding strategies using three-star recruits who develop at an average rate.[18] This popular system uses scores from -10 to +9.1 to look at instant impact players, future impact players, talent retention, in-season development, and future succession planning.

We will use the same eight factors we used previously in our probability analysis, and add a few other people or ventures in addition to Christianity, just to make it more interesting. And we will employ a scale from 1 to 10.

The first factor has to do with the built in difficulties in starting any venture or movement. Difficult, primitive conditions would give us a score of 10, whereas a modern jumping off point with plenty of high-tech advertising and marketing, could give us a ranking as low as one. Let's remember Taylor Swift. It is obviously more significant if any phenomenon begins with meager means in imperfect surroundings than in a rich, well-established vicinity. We rated all of the following eight factors on a scale from 1 to 10.

- 1. The conditions under which it was founded, primitive versus sophisticated. Primitive = maximum of 10, highly sophisticated = 1.

- 2. The amount of time it's leader spent proclaiming and developing it. The less time it took, the more significant was the outcome and higher the score.

- 3. The greater the resistance, the higher the score.
- 4. The less public relations available, the higher the score.
- 5. The number of followers today. A higher number leads to a higher score.
- 6. How long has this concept, production, or innovation lasted? The longer it has lasted, the higher the score.
- 7. The initial growth spurt, especially within the first 50 years. The faster the growth spurt, the higher the score.
- 8. The impact of this innovation on an average person's life today? Is it important and significant to many people today? The more significant, the higher the score.

Here are our initial ratings: For Christianity, all of the information used is outside the box, but for some other entities we now have the benefit of reliable information from inside the box as well. While this non-approved mathematical approach does not follow classic probability research, it is at least as objective as Sports Illustrated! If you, the reader, want to conduct your own historical research, or disagree with the weightings used for each of these factors, why don't you have some fun and substitute your own numbers?

Here are our ratings:

Christianity: eight, eight, nine, eight, ten, nine, nine, ten.

Taylor Swift: six, seven, eight, three, three, two, five, one.

Your old high school soccer team making it to the finals this year: one, one, two, three, two, two, three, two.

Donald Trump securing the Republican nomination: one, seven, six, one, four, one, four, three.

The creation of the McDonald's franchise: three, seven, two, two, four, three, six, one.

Adolf Hitler's Nazi regime: four, nine, seven, two, two, two, nine, eight.

Always doing what your family or friends want you to do: Six, five, one, four, two, two, two, and four.

The American Colonies winning the Revolutionary War, creating the most powerful country in the world, and lasting for over 200 years: Four, seven, nine, six, nine, eight, eight, nine.

Worried about grizzly bear attacks? About 130 people die each year from grizzly attacks in our national parks. Your odds of dying (if you go to one of our parks) are only 1 in 2 million.[19]

So what kind of power rating odds do we get? By simply multiplying each of the above ratings in a cumulative fashion, we came up with the objective data needed to satisfy our outside the black box research design for Christianity and both inside and outside the box information for some of the others. Here are our power ratings:

Christianity: 37 million.

Taylor Swift: 30,000.

Winning your state championship: 144.

Trump winning the Republican nomination: 2,016.

Big Mac: 6,048.

Hitler: 145,000.

Always doing what your family or friends want you to do: 3,840.

The American Colonies succeeding: 8,838,208.

You might be asking yourself what these "power ratings" actually mean. Rather than get into a fancy talk here, let's just define them by how they operate: The power ratings are no more or less than the operations needed to obtain them. Ratings from 1 to 10 over 8 categories with the higher the number the lower the probability that this person, program or idea would achieve success. These eight category numbers were then multiplied to obtain a final rating, which we are calling a power rating. The greater the magnitude of this number, the less likely it would be that the venture would succeed.

Does a power rating of 37 million mean the chances of success for Christianity were one in 37 million? A mathematical purist would object to this operational method, but it is a practical way to put a hard number on a probability factor and give us a consistent method for comparing the success of various projects.

Of course, our more scientific probability study came out with even higher odds: one in 12.5 billion. What does all of this really mean? Is the probability of the startup of Christianity and its continuing power and influence greater than other phenomena, such as the creation of our world or the evolution of human beings on earth?

We're not saying this. We are simply saying that, to the best of our knowledge, no one else has attempted to use strictly outside-of-the-box information to study the origins and growth of Christianity, and that our findings are both dramatic and commanding. How best to fit this into existing knowledge? We will stay with psychology and happily leave this discussion to theologians, philosophers, historians, and our friends in the pews.

So rather than being an obstacle to religious faith, objective research supports the idea that Christianity is not just a well-meaning myth or fairytale that cannot be looked at in an objective manner. The results of these data are so improbable that they give powerful, unquestioned weight to the conclusion that many people of faith have reached without scientific methods: that it is not smart, or scientific, to dismiss Christianity.

Chapter 11

Looking *inside* the box: what sociologists and historians can tell us.

Yes, we decided to stay *outside* the box. Our scientific approach allows us to stick to facts in order to avoid non-scientific speculation by folks who are trying to guess what's inside the box. But some of these professionals have spent years investigating biblical writings and any other information they could get their hands on in order to give us informed *speculation* into the early life of Christ and his church.

Please stay alert when you read the many books out there. They won't warn you about a hidden premise: *"We know Jesus was just a person, like you or me, so let's figure out how this man's strange cult got so big."*

One of the sociologists who has done a particularly good job of enlightening us is Rodney Stark. None other than Ken Woodward, a Notre Dame graduate and *Newsweek R*eligion editor, called it a "brilliant, fresh, blunt, and highly persuasive account of how the West was won—for Jesus."[1]

Stark does us a big favor when he reminds us of living conditions and attitudes at the time of Christ. Greco-Roman cities were slightly less than one square mile and had populations of 150,000 or more, narrow streets, and no sewage, garbage disposal, or soap. Water had to be carried in jugs.

But that was nothing compared to Roman values. Their world was saturated with cruelty and death. It was a place where wild animals tore hundreds of people apart as afternoon entertainment, and a royal boy's birthday treat was to watch the murder of innocents.

What about feminism? Women took second place or had no place prior to Christianity. Divorce, incest, marital infidelity and polygamy worked against women. Both Plato and Aristotle endorsed infanticide, and guess which gender they were eliminating? All, or nearly all of the murder of newborns were directed to females. This resulted in a population decrease similar to the recent history of China, a country also run by atheists. Abortion was also supported by the Romans and the techniques used were very dangerous.

It's too bad our priests don't review all of this when they deliver the good news in homilies. Without this context, the many nice words about helping the poor and loving one's neighbor have no bite and fall flat. Just more ho-hum stuff we've heard before. That's because we take our present Judeo-Christian culture for granted. Ross Douthat gave us his pitch to water the "plants" we've been given and keep them growing.[2]

Christianity also pushed the crazy idea that we should help the poor. In fact, the early popes were the first to institute organized help for street people. Today, the Catholic Church leads the world in charitable giving. How about visiting and caring for the sick? Another preposterous idea! The prevailing norm back then was to get rid of the weak, at birth or as soon as possible. Christian teaching about respecting and loving one another and praying to a loving God, were unheard of. Perhaps, above all, Christianity brought a new concept of humanity, a moral vision incompatible with the casual cruelty of pagan customs.

Some critics try to link the rapid growth of Christianity to Emperor Constantine's conversion to the faith. "Hey, they just got lucky." Stark's research reveals that Constantine's conversion didn't cause this. Rather, his conversion followed the massive progress already underway. He also challenges the idea that Christians did not draw from higher levels of the Roman ranking system. They drew a few highly placed folks, mostly women, but, of course, most followers would be described today as middle class or lower-middle class.

Stark even believes martyrdom had benefits for the early Church. Martyrs kept the free riders from exploiting the Church because you had to "put up or shut up." He compares this with some wealthy churches in America, where just writing a check makes you a worshiper in good standing.

Of course, some writers don't agree with Stark. Bart Ehrman, a religious studies professor at North Carolina University, has produced audio and video courses for *Great Books*. His early works took an adversarial approach and criticized the very essence of Christianity. Pity the innocent kids who took his courses in college.

More recently, he has changed his tune somewhat and takes a softer approach. His most recent book is called *The Triumph of Christianity*. In it, he traces the growth of the church to the reports of miracles. We don't know whether his thinking has changed or his publisher is seeking a wider audience.[3]

PART FOUR

Do Church Teachings Reflect Characteristics of the Brain and Central Nervous System?

Chapter 12

The Brain and the Church of Rome

ere are some impressions of the Church and how it corresponds to the brain and central nervous system. The authors were raised in the Catholic faith and their profession of neuropsychology gives them a unique view of the Church in our society.

1. In the Catholic Mass we believe we have an incredible opportunity to receive the body and blood of Jesus Christ; not just a symbol or reminder of Jesus. This belief separates us from most Protestant Churches. As we watch the priest elevate the bread and chalice of wine, we think of the hundreds of millions of Catholics who have witnessed and participated in the exact same experience we enjoy today: partaking of the bread and wine for the past 2000 years. With 28 years per generation, that equates to 70 generations!

We visualize the last time Christ met for a meal with his followers, broke the bread and raised the chalice, declaring that this was his body and blood. When we see the priest at the altar, we can see Jesus in that upper room in Jerusalem. Christ's words were too much for some of his followers, just as they are for others today.

We're not surprised that they walked away. Our understanding of the human brain gives us sympathy for those who can't accept this concept. It's radical, alright. You want cutting edge? You want something more daring than the gowns worn to the Academy Awards presentations? This is it! Kind of like coming from outer space.

As psychologists, we often use visualization as part of our treatment of chronic fears, post-traumatic stress, and training athletes for competition. So it is helpful to use one's imagination and visualize this long community chain that stretches forward from the time of Christ and touches our tongues today. The touch and the taste. This is real, folks. Real, tactile, hands on exposure, not just "book learnin'."

What Jon Hassler says about the Mass: "60 years of churchgoing has left me with a need—it's more than mere habit; it's a deep-seated need—to be lifted up and carried along, time after time, by the familiar words and rubrics. It's like boarding a boat and standing out from the shore of my life for a half hour or so, viewing it through the refreshing air of a calm and scenic harbor."[1]

Who better to point out the value of the Mass than best-selling atheist writer, Alain de Botton. He believes the Mass strengthens congregant's bonds of affection and breaks down age, social class, and other characteristics that create prejudice. What he calls a "sumptuous setting," along with the church's enormous prestige and history give the folks in the pews the confidence to connect with others.[2]

2. Catholics have a sense of humor. Have you noticed? We heard this little story in a homily (sermon) by a Franciscan priest.

A parishioner approached the priest and wanted a Mass said for his recently departed dog. The priest told the parishioner in no uncertain terms that we Catholics do not celebrate Masses for animals, only humans, and suggested she go down the street to a community church where they might conduct a service for her dog.

On the way out, the parishioner thanked him and asked the priest if he thought $5000 was enough of a contribution to the church down the street for the service—at which point the priest said "Oh, I didn't know your dog was Catholic. I'm sure I can make some arrangements for you and your blessed dog."

Yes, we like to make fun of our church. We think this reflects a mature relationship with our priests and parishioners. Have you noticed how stiff and uptight parishioners of some other churches are when they talk about God or their religious services? Yes, and we also think it's okay for adults to drink (just a little) and dance (a lot). As practitioners, we are well aware of the importance of humor in maintaining our emotional and psychological balance.

3. We also enjoy sharing our faith with the interesting people who attend our services. This is what makes the Catholic Church "catholic"—or universal. It is not confined to one country or a certain social class. Yes, we do have a few upscale parishes where wealthy people seem to congregate. But in most of our churches, you'll find the rich and the poor, college students, professors, and the mentally handicapped: all of the same kinds of people Jesus met every day in Galilee. That's why he used parables. He wanted to make sure everyone could understand him, regardless of their education or social background.

In fact, this is strong evidence of what makes our Church special. When you observe some Christian denominations, you can identify the church by the social class and the people it caters to. Some cater to the wealthy and others to the very poor. And there seems to be a church for every social category out there.

Since God's church needs to cut through all levels of humankind, we wonder if some churches have a full understanding of the gospels and the message Jesus passed along through the early church, and through our popes and saints.

All this talk about niche religions reminds us of an old joke. Can you name a type of talk therapy that exists only in New York City and Los Angeles? The answer is "on-the-couch" psychoanalysis. Since this counseling approach only existed in wealthy areas early on, then the problems must have been confined to those two cities as well. Just kidding!

Psychoanalysis helps some folks, but it is not based on science, and most farmers in West Virginia don't care for it much. By the way, the inoculation you will receive later in this book is not a niche inoculation for just folks in your town, it is universal, just as the Catholic Church is universal.

Data from the *Pew Forum on Religion and Public Life* show that Catholics in the U.S. are close to the national average in terms of income.[2b] This means that we have a balanced number of wealthy and poor people as well as those in between.

The fact that some religious denominations attract a narrower segment of the population doesn't mean they aren't good Christians or are lacking in faith, but it is important, in our view, to be catholic (universal) as well as Catholic.

4. Ours is a church of sinners, and we psychologists fit right in! Some churches seem to have little room for sinners, whereas we believe our church is a church of, for, and about, sinners. And most

of us folks in the pews know the human race is flawed. There's that original sin again!

"As Jesus was walking along, he saw a man called Matthew sitting at the tax booth; and he said to him, 'Follow me.' And he got up and followed him.

"And as he sat at dinner in the house, many tax collectors and sinners came and were sitting with him and his disciples. When the Pharisees saw this they said to his disciples, 'Why does your teacher eat with tax collectors and sinners?'

"But when he heard this, he said, 'Those who are well have no need of a physician, but those who are sick do. Go and learn what this means, I desire mercy, not sacrifice. For I have come to call not the righteous but sinners.'"[3]

What if we discover a life-saving medication, but only distribute it to people who are not sick or have only minor symptoms? Discouraging roughnecks, weirdos, and bad guys from your church makes for a happy and smooth-running religious community, but doesn't it defeat the true purpose of Christ's redemptive spirit?

Pope Francis, in his 2016 book, *The Name of God is Mercy*, says we should never challenge Jesus' message of unconditional love and mercy for even the most wretched of sinners. "We must avoid the attitude of someone who judges and condemns from the lofty heights of his own certainty."[4]

5. Speaking of Pope Francis, the authors really like having a Church leader who is an international celebrity, and the really cool thing about our Church leader is that his celebrity status continues through the ages. Some people are critical of the pope, but when a pope visits the United States, or any country for that matter, the turnout is phenomenal. In 2015, despite heavy rain, Pope Francis

drew 6 million to a Mass in Manila, Philippines, one the largest turnouts for a single event in the history of the world.[5]

But not all popes are appreciated. Catholic historian Gary Wills is rather critical of our first pope, Peter. "He is a comic boaster who bungles everything. His fourth century supporters, as we shall see, tried to make him a Moses. The Gospels make him less a Moses than a Mr. Magoo. A man of action, he invariably takes the wrong action."[6]

Is the pope Catholic? We think this humorous description of Peter defines him as Catholic through and through. *Just another sinner who tries very hard to do the right thing.* Sometimes other churches have leaders, or at least preachers, who gain worldwide celebrity status. Who can ever forget Billy Graham's missions?

A Southern Baptist Minister, Graham, held large indoor and outdoor rallies that were attended over the years by approximately 215 million people. We Catholics have had some great speakers, too. St. John Chrysostom was called "golden-mouthed," back in 349-407 AD. With our popes, we Catholics are fortunate to have a revered, perennial leader, and preacher—through the ages.

6. The way our church services have developed over the past 2000 years is yet another clue to the truth and soundness of the Catholic Church. We authors study and deal with the brain and behavior. Research in the last 30 years or so has allowed us to study different areas of the brain. Some are logical and verbal, less reliant on visual images or creative and inspirational ideas. Other parts of the brain emphasize emotions and the creative processes.

The completeness and richness of our Catholic services encourage us to enjoy and benefit from all of these characteristics. Homilies (sermons), music, incense, and works of art represent the complexity and richness of the brain, whereas some other groups seem to draw on limited areas of the brain, just as they have aligned themselves with various social classes or narrower aspects of human experience. In other words, we are inclusive and function in a way that represents us all.

The opportunity for visual input at our Mass includes paintings, statues, and incredibly beautiful stained glass windows. Incense appeals to the sense of smell and delivers clouds of rising perfumed smoke, which sometimes seems to assume the shape of Jesus and the saints. Holy water reminds us of John the Baptist and our own baptism. Catholic priests wear history-inspired robes that offer visual memories of the time of Christ, and reflect our changing religious seasons.

Some early reformers believed, or wanted to believe that Catholics were actually *worshiping* these paintings, statues, and other works of art. So these Kings and reformers stripped churches of everything that represented saints or other great church leaders. In our opinion, this is a rather condescending attitude toward Catholics.

In secular art, when we love a painting such as the "Mona Lisa" or the statue "The Thinker," we are showing our appreciation for its beauty and for its creator, in these cases Da Vinci and Rodin, respectively. Our Catholic art is a powerful reminder of God and his followers. If churchgoers actually worship an inanimate object, they must have emotional or mental problems.

During the reign of Henry VIII in England, reformers destroyed every religious image found in English churches and cathedrals. They chiseled the names of saints from church walls (this is where the term "chiseler" comes from). In 2013, the Tate Britain Museum in London, England, featured the histories of British image destroyers.

Some of the pieces had never been displayed in public before, including the statue of the dead Christ, circa 1500 – 1520, which survived the violent destruction of these religious reformers. It shows

Christ removed from the cross: the crown of thorns, arms and lower legs missing "at the hands of protesting image destroyers."[7] When Henry VIII, Oliver Cromwell, and other reformers finished their work, they had destroyed over 90% of all of the art in England prior to 1560!

7. We love and respect our priests. Our psychological evaluations of priesthood candidates over the past 35 years have made us realize just how special these people are. This was covered in more detail in chapter four, where we discussed how priesthood applicants coped with psychological testing and what their psychological profiles revealed.

Because of their solid faith, most priests are able to celebrate the humorous "Trinity" of eating, drinking, and praying. The father of one of the authors, who was, of course, the grandfather of the junior author, was a traveling salesman in the South in the 1940s. He often commented on the hypocrisy of the "Damnation Preachers."

While E.A. Hicks, the father and grandfather of the authors, rarely attended church, he respected Catholic priests because he saw them as open and natural, and believed they didn't take themselves too seriously. At the same time, this same E.A. Hicks wouldn't let the senior author, as a child, watch Catholic seminarians play softball, because in the heat of a tight game a seminarian might cough up an occasional "hell" or "damn."

Another revealing story about Catholic priests concerns Father Francis McIntyre, a U.S. Air Force chaplain who baptized the junior author. The officer's club at Bentwaters Royal Air Force Station (RAF) in Suffolk, England brought in a "professional dancer" from a London nightclub a couple of times a year to entertain the pilots and support personnel. Prince Philip even showed up for one of the performances.

Every minister at the base found a better place to be on that evening. But Father McIntyre stayed at the club bar, a room separate from where the "dancer" was performing, so that he could listen to the concerns of the young pilots. Needless to say, he was a highly respected and popular priest. Was this scandalous behavior on his part? He didn't think so. Neither do we.

8. As mentioned earlier, our Mass is a place separate from our daily lives; a place that allows us to imagine our spiritual future. A refuge. A place of gathering. A place of inspirational words from the Old and New Testaments. A place that taps all areas of the brain. Sometimes, when we are having a special Mass, we pull out all the stops to enjoy a full choir, incense, and a sprinkling of all congregants with holy water. We Catholics joke about this service by referring to it as "bells and smells."

There we go again, making fun of our own Church. We must feel pretty confident that we have the whole package. Right? Other folks sometimes make fun of Catholics and we enjoy their humor as well. We saw a poster on a website with the following message, referring to Catholics at Mass: "Stand up, sit down, kneel, stand, and now sit again. Anyone for a coffee break?"

We enjoy that humor, but research into physiology and brain function demonstrate increased concentration and brain stimulation when physical activity accompanies thinking and visual perception. Once again, the Church managed to discover a positive brain-related approach long before science turned its attention to these matters. And all this moving around gives our kids something to do—especially some of our fidgety little boys—bless them.

Chapter 13

Neuropsychology and the Three Brains

Robert Ornstein helped us understand how the two sides of the brain see things differently. One (the left brain) focuses on small elements and links them together so they can be reproduced like a formula. The other (the right brain) links together the large strokes of a life.[1]

As Robert Sapolsky points out in his review of biology and human behavior, this concept is correct even though subtle.[2] Recent research shows that all parts of the brain are needed in all brain activities including thinking and feeling. In fact, a 2016 study showed that the brain may work as a word cloud, with a much more extensive landscape of meaning that covers both sides of the brain and lower brain centers.[3]

Left Brain descriptors: Literal, content, sequential thinking, linear, bottom-up-thinking, sequential progression, logical, language, facts, and control.

Right brain descriptors: Imaginative, expansive, nonlinear, top-down thinking, prioritize, epiphany and intuitive, and movement.

Some folks also designate a third brain and this has to do with lower brain centers that involve instincts, raw energy and renewal.

In the author's view, some people seem to have rather extreme "left-brain" personalities. They are literal in their thinking and use facts and logic at the expense of imagination, intuition, and a sense of wonder. These "technicians" reduce everything to logic and facts, and seem to have a strong need for control. It's easy to see how they could reject the concept of God. If we authors relied entirely on left-brain thinking, we'd probably agree that this country bumpkin named Jesus couldn't really be God.

In fact, the belief that Jesus is God is illogical, and logic is what left brainers rely on almost completely. The irony here is that if we were able to reason our way to understanding all about God, then we, in fact, would be God. No, right brain intuition and imagination must be blended with left brain logic to get the big picture.

Harry Harlow proved that curiosity is a basic human drive, yet a small percentage of people seem to lack curiosity, creativity, or a sense of wonder about the world.[4] They are smothered by detail and hard facts. Since only 4-5% of the population falls in the atheist camp, should we consider them as lacking in right brain functions? (Note to our agnostic friends—only kidding. We think you're just developmentally delayed and will eventually see the big picture. Ha.)

Remember Adam and Eve? They lived in a lower-brain and right-brain paradise, cavorting like children. God warned them about the left-brained tree of knowledge, and showed a special love for children.

Some folks fear that left-brain scientists are destroying the very essence of the way we see the world. Biochemist Erwin Chargaff:

"This wonderful, inconceivably intricate tapestry is being taken apart strand by strand; each thread pulled out, torn up, and analyzed; and at the end even the memory of the design is lost and can no longer be recalled."[5]

We also find folks within the religious community offering different brain views of the spiritual world. The bumper sticker, "My (right brain) Karma Ran over Your (left brain) Dogma," says it all.

In writing about cooperation between religion and science in *Life is a Miracle*, Wendell Berry could be describing the two sides of the brain and the competition between them. "Both imagination and a competent sense of reality are necessary to our life, and they necessarily discipline one another. They should cease to be 'two cultures' and become fully communicating, if not always fully cooperating, parts of one culture."[6]

Brain history is a kind of miracle. It's really interesting to note that knowledge of left and right brain differences were identified long before modern fMRI studies and split-brain research: They were found in Psychiatrist Eric Bern's theory of TA (Transactional Analysis) which proposed three ways humans operate: Adult, Parent and Child. The Adult is rational, gathers information, and is not impulsive (read left brain). The Parent deals more with the ideal than the factual and draws on traditional, worldviews (read right brain). The Child is closer to instincts and basic physiological processes (read lower-brain centers).[7]

Even before Bern, Sigmund Freud proposed that the personality is made up of three major systems: The Id, the Ego and the Superego. The Id holds our mental energy and furnishes all of the power for the operation of the other two systems (read lower brain centers). The Ego has control over our thinking and obeys the factual, reality principle (read left brain). The Superego represents the ideal rather than the real and focuses on the traditional, inspirational values of society (read right brain).

Our research led us to wonder if anyone else had come up with this brilliant concept. Yes, no surprise here—the good old Catholic Church. Long, long before today's fMRIs, Eric Bern, and Sigmund Freud, the Church indorsed the religious concept of the *Trinity*.

God the Father corresponds to the Adult, Ego, or left-brain that lays out the commandments and dogma of the church. The Holy Spirit is the Parent, Superego, or right-brain that speaks in tongues of fire and is inspirational. The Son of God corresponds to lower-brain centers bringing forth rebirth, renewal, and energy—God-made-flesh.

It's truly amazing to think that ancient Catholic monks, without the help of fMRIs or computers, were able to come up with this complex concept. Maybe the Holy Spirit had a couple of Ph.D.'s. in neuroscience and slipped them a few hints. What do you think?

PART FIVE

The Devil's Laboratory:
Media and Pop Psychology

Chapter 14

There's a sucker born every minute.
Buyer beware: "Snake Bites Man,
Man Bites His Wife!" Wow!

In this era of "fake news," it's a good idea to carefully evaluate what we are seeing, hearing, and reading. Can we rely on newspaper "truth" meters? One of the first things a business student learns in college is the age-old warning: *caveat emptor,* or buyer beware. Yes, some unscrupulous sales folks will use unethical and misleading claims to make a sale. P.T. Barnum of circus fame warned us that "there is a sucker born every minute."[1]

How do we know when we are being misled? For starters, we should prepare ourselves for the *Wow* effect. When a headline makes us react with Wow, we are probably about to be misled. Here's one that is rather obvious: "Snake Bites Man, Man Bites His Wife." Wow! It's pretty catchy, and of course the story isn't at all what we were led to think. It's the alleged story of a man who thought he would die from a snake bite and wanted his wife to join him in the next world.[2]

Here's another tip: We recommend checking out the last three paragraphs of any story with a Wow headline. Journalists will often wait until the end of an article to tone down their exaggerated headlines and balance their marginal claims with the truth. This can save us a lot of time.

We feel that we got the *Wow* results from our outside the box research on the origins of Christianity, but we didn't headline it and we think we can back up the results.

Most of the headlines that we have difficulty with are subtler than the snake story. "Christians Faced Widespread Harassment in 2015, but mostly in Christian Majority Countries." This might lead us to think that Christians are being harassed—by other Christians! In fact, the story is simply pointing out that more harassment of all kinds takes place in very large countries than in smaller ones because there are more people. Tricky, wouldn't you say?[3]

How about this one? "The Teenage Spiritual Crisis." We might think from this headline that teenagers do not believe in God, but the article goes on to point out that most teens are believers. In fact, they report that 84% of 13 to 17-year-olds believe in God.[4] But that headline certainly got our attention. And of course, elsewhere in this book, we mentioned a poll asserting that fewer religious people are going to church, but later it was revealed that Catholics were not included in the poll.

Here's a similar one: "More Australians Now Identify as Non-religious." So, does this mean that most Australians are not religious? No, the article goes on to say that 30% of the young people questioned were non-religious, and this was after a large influx of non-Europeans.

Also, this census is given every five years, but the data used for comparison was 16 years old. Our conclusion is that this little bit of non-news was cooked, basted, fried, and grilled—all for our benefit.[5]

Figures don't lie, but liars figure? Here's the mother of gaming the system. According to Joe Flint, a writer for *The Wall Street Journal,* NBC hides their low-rated TV shows by changing the spelling of "NBC Nightly News" to "NBC Nitely News," to fool the Nielsen computer which is used to rate shows. Sometimes being a poor speller comes in handy![6]

We are also influenced by the size of headlines and where they are positioned in the newspaper. If we see a modest headline near the back of the paper, we are inclined to assume the story is not that important. If the newspaper has a bias, and many do, this is one way of using a headline to editorialize without giving us the paper's official editorial opinion in the editorial section—where it belongs.

One newspaper had three headlines near each other. "Mattis stresses integrity to grads," "Pope speaks out against abortion," and "22-FOOT-LONG PYTHON SWALLOWS WOMAN WHOLE." (Wow). The python headline was in caps and bold, while the other two were small, lower case, and of equal size.[7]

It's not just headlines, either. Sometimes articles in the news section of the paper are really editorials. For example, in an article about the firing of Michael T. Flynn, former U.S. National Security Advisor, it states that "Flynn is a man who is *seething* and *thwarted* and after repeatedly *clashing* with other officials, decided that the military's loss would be his gain and he would *parlay* his contacts and *disdain* for conventional bureaucracy, etc. etc."[8] (Our italics)

Is this simply a news article? We have highlighted the opined words to emphasize the editorial aspects of this "news" report. Unless the reporters can get inside Mr. Flynn's head and have extensive training in psychology, they are giving biased opinions, not news, and negative ones at that.

So it is truly *buyer beware* out there.

How about an editorial on the front page of the newspaper that uses no print and says nothing but still conveys a powerful message? When TV talk show host Bill O'Reilly was accused of sexual misconduct it made headlines in many newspapers. One paper chose to include a large picture on the front page of the next day's paper showing Pope Francis shaking hands with Mr. O'Reilly.[9] Of course, the pope's white robe signifies purity and the warm handshake is a sign of trust and welcome. It seemed to be saying "welcome aboard Mr. Sex Abuser."

We need to ask ourselves, what is the message here? If it's news, what does it mean? If it's an editorial, why isn't it on the editorial page? Of course, the picture was taken long before there were any accusations against O'Reilly.

Who gets on the front page, anyway? Annually, 103 million folks attend sporting events so they should be on the front page. Right? Hold it. Attendance at religious events exceeds 5.6 billion.[10]

Can misleading opinions affect our culture in a negative way? Let's remember, P.T. Barnum is still out there, and the modern P.T. Barnum would like nothing more than to bring down the Catholic Church, the backbone of Christianity. *We don't want to be his suckers.*

Chapter 15

Sticking With the Facts. Getting the Real Deal.

Yes, "buyer beware" is still prevalent today. We have to wonder how immigrants coming to the United States manage to sort through all the media and advertising "tricks" they're subjected to. Maybe, if we just had the basic facts, we wouldn't be misled, or so we think. But sometimes the facts can be difficult to uncover and can mislead us as well.

A group of anthropologists wanted to study native life in a number of African villages. They sent researchers to take notes and record their observations. When the observers returned to their university in the States, scientists discovered significant differences in their notes. The professors decided to solve the problem by using video recordings. This would give them facts without any personal interpretations and bring researchers closer to the truth.

Another team followed up with video cameras. When given the new data, the professors were disappointed with the vast array of conflicting film footage they received. Finally, they came to the conclusion that *it's where you point the camera that counts*. So facts aren't as easy to come by as we might think.[1]

Another example comes from World War II when military researchers attempted to determine which pilots were most effective in combat. Getting the true facts about what happened in combat would help them train future pilots. Up until that time, researchers had relied on pilots' recollections under highly stressful conditions of combat. They decided to install cameras in the noses of the fighter aircraft to get the solid evidence they needed.[2]

Sure enough, they were able to tell which pilots attacked the most enemy planes and which pilots had the highest hit rates. They were satisfied with this factual information and were about to turn the results over to the war department when a lower grade officer pointed out something that hadn't occurred to them.

In the fighter command they were studying, the fighters flew as a team with one pilot designated as the gunner and the other three pilots assigned to set up the operation and provided protection. As a result, the gunner would almost always have the most productivity, whether he was the best pilot or not. The researchers had to go back to the drawing board. Once again, facts can be elusive.

Pop psychology and some agnostic scientists want us to believe the world can be divided into fact and values, and *facts are what counts*. The problem with this is that (in fact) values determine what we will pay attention to and what will count as a fact.[3]

If facts are so elusive, why don't we just set up a fact-finding program that will tell us what is true and what is false? This would improve our understanding of the news and save us a lot of time. It just so happens that we do have fact-finding services. In fact, the authors counted approximately 15 sites that promise to dig deep and give us only the facts.[4] One of them even has a truth meter. The story or comment under question registers either true or false or mostly true or mostly false on the picture of a meter. What could be easier?[5]

Wait a minute. How do we know the fact finders aren't biased? One organization found 40 or 50 patterns of deception that we should be aware of when taking in the news, but what if the fact-finders-themselves are falling into patterns of deception?[6] If the fact-checking group is run by editors and reporters of a newspaper, aren't they likely to be biased in the direction of their employers? After all, their jobs may be on the line.

It's important to know the funding source of a fact checker, and it's critical that they use neutral wording and have unbiased sources check out their facts. Another problem with using editors and reporters is that they are not scientists and may not comprehend the truth even though they can pin down the facts.

For example, one critic showed possible bias by a well-known fact checker. Presidential candidate Mitt Romney said the United States government was spending 42% of the economy on government services. These fact-checking organizations decided that Romney's numbers didn't tell the whole story because the checkers were of the opinion that Social Security, Medicare, and Medicaid, shouldn't count as current government spending! As a result, they rated Romney's statement as only mostly true, but this critic believed the rating should have been true.[7]

Similar to the study using cameras in Africa, if a fact checking organization is biased, it's very easy for them to select those articles where misstatements make their opponent look bad and omit misstatements by the person or organization they support. They can also make a small, inconsequential statement seem quite important and relevant. As with headline placement, the impact depends on where the fact checker article appears and how much space it takes up.

What if research is unbiased and we are getting the true facts? Can we finally relax and accept what scientists tell us about the results? That may not be the case. Now, we are faced with *interpretation* of facts and research, and that's where bias can still creep in.

Here's an example: Some of the world's finest scientists of the twentieth century did work on genetics, but one man, Konrad Lorenz, interpreted these findings to support his own prejudices. Lorenz was a brilliant scientist and Nobel Laureate who was a regular guest on nature TV programs.

Lorenz joined the Nazi Party and worked to psychologically screen people of German and Polish parentage to determine which ones were sufficiently German to be spared death. His misinterpretation of the impact of genes on humans led him to believe that "socially inferior" humans would destroy society and should be exterminated.[8] This false interpretation, of course, supported the Nazi mindset.

Looking at the same research, another respected scientist, behavioral psychologist John Watson, took an opposite view to that of Lorenz. He believed that behavior was completely changeable as long as one has the right environment. He thought he could take any person and train that person to be or do anything.

We now know that people are not born with the same potential and attributes. Any parent with more than one child can testify to these differences. Watson's faulty interpretation of research still influences us today. Teachers are blamed when their students' test scores are low, for example, but we need to recognize that not all students have the same basic abilities.[9]

So getting the correct facts can be difficult, and once we have them we still need to question how best to interpret them.

Chapter 16

Research Made Simple

First, how are we using the term research? People can simply go to Goggle and look up information on a subject and say they did research. The authors think of that as merely information seeking.

At a deeper and move valid level, historians and other professors will study a subject and apply some *general* research strategies. One example of this is found in Rodney Stark's book, *The Rise of Christianity.*[1] Stark calculates the number of Christians in the year A.D. 300 by looking at the *estimates* given by other historians earlier on and then adding larger numbers each year until he reaches a conclusion in the year 300. He then applies some statistical measures to better understand these figures. This is an educated estimate, but is not modern laboratory research.

At its deepest level, scientific research requires controlling the entities or things compared, and then applying statistical measures to make sure results are reliable and valid. This is the author's research

117

which we reported on in Part Three. It relied on laboratory techniques and statistics acceptable to the scientific community. Often, journalists will couch their investigations in scientific terms or call it research, but that does not mean they are utilizing laboratory science. This is confusing for writers and book editors as well.

We have demonstrated in Part four of this book how we can use controlled laboratory science to examine the life of Christ without any reliance on experts who must use marginal and often unreliable formation from "inside the box."

Can we always rely on this laboratory research to discover truth? Unfortunately not. While science is our best way to answer "what" questions (vs. questions involving religion and the supernatural) it is still susceptible to error because scientists and their followers are subject to human limitations. Rather than simply list those errors, we have compiled a list of recent research studies that went wrong:

- Support for meds for depression was overstated because the publisher was publishing only the positive studies and the project was funded by the drug industry.[2]
- The Nation's Report Card showed good results for a county in Florida when compared to "equivalent" schools elsewhere, but the schools weren't equivalent or even similar. They had widely different poverty rates.[3]
- A professor at Stanford University is suing a fellow researcher for critiquing his work incorrectly.[4]
- Fifty years ago, researcher Paul Ehrich said the population explosion would destroy much of the world by 2018.[5]
- The National Institute of Health spent 100 million on research to show that moderate use of alcohol was beneficial, but there was intentional bias and secret interactions with the alcohol industry.[6]

- A new psychological test measures unconscious roots of prejudice in most people, but the test lacked reliability and is therefore not valid.[7]
- A jury required Monsanto to pay $289 million for not warning consumers about *Roundup*, which the jury thought caused cancer, but research evidence shows that glyphosate in *Roundup* doesn't cause cancer.[8]
- Research on a new drug to treat NEODOO1 was stopped when it was discovered that subjects receiving placebo (phony pills containing no medicine) did better than those receiving the medication.[9]
- The EPA stopped publishing studies from third parties because they weren't getting the methods and data—only the conclusions.[10]
- A *New England Journal of Medicine* blood pressure study (Sprint) showed 25% reduction in cardiovascular deaths, but it turns out that was only a 2% difference and subjects had a higher-than-average risk for heart events.[11]
- Cancer treatment ads rely on emotion while leaving out useful research information.[12]
- The chief medical officer at Sloan Kettering Cancer Research center failed to disclose payments of over $3 million from drug and health care companies.[13]
- A leading researcher at Cornell University lost his job when he was accused of fraud by people in his lab. HARKing is when a study is run and then *after* it is finished the authors decide what was being studied.[14]
- "A broken system" allows medical journals to have a relationship with researchers who publish in their newspapers.[15]

So what did we learn from this sampling of recent studies? Researchers shouldn't publish *just* the studies that support their position. Studies must be repeatable or they can't be valid. When comparing two things, we must have a level playing field. We need to stick to the facts, and not emotion.

We have to be suspicious when the study is funded by industry. The study must be repeated by others who are completely independent of the original researchers (replication). When two things go together it doesn't mean that A caused B (correlation) because maybe B caused A, or C caused them both. Funds received from private industry must be disclosed.

So be careful when you see or hear the words—"the research shows." It probably does, but not always.

Chapter 17

No room at the Inn for Blacks, Irish, or dogs. Avoiding myths and hysteria. How do witch-hunts start and why do people support them?

Sarah Good and four other defendants were hanged on July 19, 1692. An 18-year-old accuser said that Sarah Good's spirit abused her. That's right, not Sarah herself, but her spirit. This was all part of the Salem Witch Trials. Could this kind of hysteria still exist today? No doubt. And it often begins with myths.[1]

Myths? A good example is the negativity generated toward Catholic immigrants in the mid-800s and early 1900s. The Irish were stereotyped as uncivilized, unskilled, and impoverished.

Many ads for employment stated "no Irish, no Blacks, no dogs." There was support for policies that would limit Irish political power, including the right to vote or hold public office. Irish women were described as "reckless breeders" because they had larger families than the locals, and it was believed that Catholics had a major political allegiance to the pope. Arsonists destroyed a Catholic convent in Philadelphia and this finally led Catholics to build their own schools.[1b]

One consequence of all this prejudice and hysteria was the Blaine amendment. James G. Blaine was a congressman who later ran for president of the United States. This amendment basically states that no money raised by taxation in any state shall ever find its way to religious institutions.

The Blaine Amendment is the current law in many states. As recently as 2016 this amendment was used in Nevada to oppose educational savings accounts that would help parents pay tuition at non-public schools.[2]

Fear of Catholic loyalty to the Vatican dogged the governor of New York, Alfred E. Smith, in his bid to become a presidential nominee in 1928. Smith was finally nominated, but he was defeated in his run for the presidency. It also dogged the candidacy of John F. Kennedy in 1960.

Kennedy decided to address this issue head on and asked if America was going to "admit to the world that a Jew can be elected mayor of Dublin, a Protestant can be chosen foreign minister of France, and a Moslem can be elected to the Israeli parliament, but a Catholic cannot be president of the United States?" He went on to win the presidency.[3]

More recently, in May, 2018, Father Patrick Conroy was removed as chaplain of the U.S. House of Representatives and told that he was being replaced by a non-Catholic because he prayed that a new tax law would be equitable for all citizens. Father Conroy had also had conversations about anti-Catholic prejudice in Congress. He was eventually reinstated.[3b]

Another whiff of anti-Catholic sentiment took place during the volatile questioning of Supreme Court nominee, Bret Cavanaugh in October, 2018. Pointed and repeated references to Cavanaugh's attendance at an exclusive Catholic high school, founded by the Jesuits, seemed to imply an *association* between the candidates' alleged failings and his Catholic background and culture.[4]

In December, 2018, a black, Pentecostal minister defended a nominee for judgeship on a U.S. District Court when two powerful U.S. senators wanted the nominee to explain his membership in a group that took "extreme positions." The group? The Knights of Columbus, a Catholic service organization that raises millions for charities, defends minorities, and fought the Ku Klux Klan.[4b]

Media persecution? On January 18, 2019, a group of protestors confronted Catholic high school students who were visiting Washington D.C. A leading newspaper headlined the event: "Boys in 'Make America Great Again" Hats Mob Native Elder at Indigenous Peoples March." After careful review, it was apparent that the school boys had done nothing wrong. Their only offense was that they were "apparently Trump supporters, and Catholic."[4c] Journalists need to regain their patience, objectivity and professionalism.

One interesting episode, especially for Catholics, took place 95 years ago, on May 17, 1924. Nowhere in America was the Ku Klux Klan stronger than in Indiana. In 1924, about one in three white men in Indiana were members of the Klan. The Klan's newspaper, *The Fiery Cross*, announced a week-long "Clavern" near the University of Notre Dame in South Bend, Indiana.

Klansmen looked on Notre Dame as a symbol of rising Catholic power in America. When the first Klansmen stepped off the train in South Bend, a crowd of angry students met them and forced them back onto the train. Clashes took place throughout the weekend and thousands of students massed downtown to battle the Klan. Notre Dame President Fr. Matthew Walsh managed to calm the crowd and prevent further violence.[5]

Gordon's story: Some older folks will recognize the name Gordon MacRae and perhaps confuse it with Gordon McRae, the popular singer who starred in the Broadway musical *Oklahoma!* The Gordon MacRae we're discussing today was born in Beverly, Massachusetts in 1953 and in 1994 was sentenced to 34 to 67 years in the New Hampshire State Prison for Men.

This Gordon MacRae is a Catholic priest. He attended Lynn, Mass. public schools through high school and was then employed as a machinist. At the age of 20 he received his calling to the priesthood. He earned a degree in psychology with honors in 1978 and studied theology at St. Mary's Seminary from 1978 to 1981.[6]

According to reporter Dorothy Rabinowitz, Fr. MacRae was convicted by a jury and imprisoned based on the claims of a single accuser who had a history of forgery, assault, theft and drug use. In 1994, the then-27-years-old accuser claimed that Fr. MacRae sexually assaulted him over five consecutive weekly counseling sessions in 1983, when he was 15 years old. Asked why he would repeatedly return to a place where he had been brutally attacked the week before, Grover testified that he "had experienced 'out of body' episodes" that had blocked his recollection" of previous abuse.[7]

Multiple, independent sources said the accuser had admitted privately that he was never assaulted by MacRae. He said he had accused the priest in order to sue the Church for money. Other accusers said they were coerced by law enforcement officials to falsely implicate MacRae.

A courtroom witness claimed that a therapist, hired by the accuser's lawyer, used hand signals from the back of the courtroom during the trial in order to coach the accuser on the witness stand. A veteran FBI agent who conducted a three-year investigation found no evidence that MacRae committed the crimes he was charged with, or any other crimes.

MacRae passed a lie detector test (polygraph) on two occasions, but the prosecutor refused to look at the results because they were not permissible in court. Finally, the prosecution offered a plea deal of 1 to 3 years if Fr. MacRae would admit to any one of the charges against him. He adamantly refused, stating that he had done nothing wrong. Subsequently sentenced to what was the equivalent of a life sentence, McRae is still in prison.

Is MacRae innocent? We don't know, but based on all the evidence, it appears likely. The real lesson to be taken from this shocking story, however, is the hysteria that can undermine objective and impartial evidence.

Sexual abuse of a minor is a horrible crime. We'd all feel a lot better about ourselves and our Church if no priest had ever been involved in that despicable use of power to hurt others and satisfy twisted needs. At the same time, it's important to have an objective view of what actually happened.

In the 64 years between 1950 and May 3, 2014, there were 3,637 credible accusations made against priests. During that same time there were 110,000 priests active in ministry during that half a century of activity. While we won't make excuses for this sinful behavior, we can see that it involved a small percentage of priests.[8] In February, 2019, the much publicized grand jury report actually documented a decline in current cases. Every one of the accused priests was either deceased or had been removed from ministry, and only two had been accused of abusing a child in the last 20 years.[8b]

Mark Clayton, staff writer for the Christian Science Monitor, reported that over a 17-year period, between 1985 and 2002, 70 clerics were sentenced to prison for child sexual abuse. Of this group, 38 were Roman Catholic priests, and the other ministers were Methodists, Baptists, Pentecostals, and Episcopal priests.[9] CBS news pointed out that members of non-religious professions were also guilty of sexually abusing minors. This includes the Boy Scouts, U.S.A. Gymnastics, and Penn State University.

Under the mandates of President George W. Bush's "No Child Left Behind Act," 2002, the Federal Department of Education carried out a study of sexual abuse in America's school systems. Hofstra University researcher Carol Shakeshaft concluded that physical sexual abuse of students in schools was likely more than *100 times greater than abuse by priests.* This federal report said that 422,000 California public school students would be victims before graduation—a number much greater than the state's entire Catholic school enrollment of 143,000.

"Despite this, in the first half of 2002, the 61 largest newspapers in California ran nearly 2000 stories about sexual abuse in Catholic institutions, mostly concerning past allegations. During that same period, newspapers ran only four stories about the federal government's discovery of the much larger and ongoing abuse scandal in the public schools."[10]

In May of 2017, the State of Texas reported 222 cases of improper relationships between public school teachers and their students. Under a new law, administrators who help sexual offenders get a job at their school merely *risk* having their state teaching certificate revoked. If that number held true for the time period used to study priest offenses, 64 years, it would amount to 14,000 cases in only one of our fifty states, albeit a large one.[11]

Not all accusations are true. Because of the Catholic Church's size and the way it is structured, it has more wealth under one roof than many small, independent, neighborhood churches. Sometimes "deep pockets" draw lawsuits—for obvious reasons. Does this mean that most accusers were out to make money? No, but all factors need to be assessed if we're to stick with an objective analysis. As long as the Church is centrally organized in terms of its finances, and lawyers need to make a living, negative newspaper accounts will continue.

On June 5, 2016, Pope Francis issued new guidelines to rid the church of those who have been negligent in handling child and adult abuse. Bishops who have not properly investigated sex abuse cases are being investigated by four Vatican offices. If they are found to be negligent, "they will be removed in order to protect those who are the weakest among the persons entrusted to them."[12]

This makes it easier for bishops to be removed, but some directors of survivor's networks are skeptical about enforcement. When the Church handles policies directly without putting them in writing, it is accused of covering up. Even when it makes its policies explicit, in written form, the perception remains that the Church doesn't enforce them. It's kind of hard to win, wouldn't you say? In September of 2018, Pope Francis called the largest meeting ever of church leaders to address sexual abuse.

Will these sex investigation networks continue to draw headlines? People who start organizations to support a certain cause rarely disband when they have accomplished their mission. It's rare because it is human nature to keep the project going. There is great ego investment in any group's day-to-day functioning and success.

This scandalous behavior reminds the authors of another nationally-hyped case of child abuse. In the late 1980s, counselors reported that some of their patients had been abused in daycare centers, but had repressed memories of these abuses. It was finally concluded, after many daycare owners and workers were tried and convicted, that this was mainly the result of counselors who were encouraging false memories through suggestion. Research shows that some kids and adults are highly suggestible and others are not.

New research in 2015 shows how memories become distorted. Memory is easy to manipulate, so researchers planted false memories in people's minds to explore eye-witness testimony in criminal trials."[13] Sure enough, the subjects in the study took on the false memories.

Elizabeth Loftus' research study planted false memories by simply showing them posters of Disney characters, including Mikey Mouse and Bugs Bunny. Many subjects later remembered meeting Bugs Bunny on a trip to Disney World, and some even said Bugs touched them inappropriately. There was one big problem: Bugs Bunny isn't a Disney character.[14]

All of this daycare hysteria came to an end when the United States Supreme Court struck down a California measure that retroactively extended the statute of limitations for molestation cases. The ruling stated that, "the 1994 law was passed during an era of hysteria over repressed memory and satanic ritual abuse."[15] Some children were probably abused in daycare settings, but when hysteria prevails, an accurate assessment is almost impossible.

Another factor is our secular culture. This is no excuse for molestation of any kind, but secular media seems ambivalent about pedophilia (children as preferred sexual objects). Our culture seems to enjoy "pedophilia chic"—from Calvin Klein underwear ads to mainstream defenses of the North American Man-Boy Love Association."[16]

In February, 2019, McDonald's and Nestlé SA withdrew advertising when a YouTube video showed inappropriate user comments about underage girls in compromising positions. Two million viewers watched the videos.[16b]

One of the authors of this book received an ad from The Folio Society of Great Britain for the book *Lolita*. Bound in leather, this best seller was selling for $99.95 and is about a middle-aged man's sexual obsession with a 12-year-old girl. The Folio Society boasted that "Lolita is rightly hailed as one of the richest and most ingenious linguistic achievements of the 20th century." Another book, *The Vagina Monologues* included the seduction and statutory rape of a young woman by an older woman, but made the rounds of many Catholic and secular universities.

Even if some concerned people exaggerated this abuse scandal as a way of criticizing the Church or for financial reward, the other part of the problem was the belief that Catholic Bishops moved priests from one geographical area to another, in order to hide their crimes.

Apparently, some bishops did move their problem priests, but fifty years ago, it was believed that psychotherapy and medication could help these tortured souls. The recommendation, from mental health professionals, including one of the authors of this book, was to give them psychotherapy and medication and move them to new geographic settings where they could start fresh and focus on their treatment.

In hindsight, a half century later, and with current knowledge about the difficulty of changing this behavior, this was not the best of advice. It often didn't help the victim or the predator, and inadvertently minimized the degree and scope of the overall problem. It was, however, the accepted professional standard at that time.

In the 1970's, the authors can recall a psychiatrist who was abusing children in his hospital-clinic in Florida and the treatment plan was for a few months of counseling and medication before reassigning him to California—to direct a children's treatment center!

The sinful behavior of others does not alleviate the guilt of Catholic priests one bit, but it is important to look at the facts and not just hysterical reactions in order to better judge the Catholic Church's role in this ugly and damaging episode.

How do witch-hunts start and why do people support them? An academic paper by Timur Kuran suggests that *availability* of information from recognized sources starts a "cascade" of belief. It's easier to go along with media or gossip if it agrees with our own biases. There is also the fear of being out of step with prevailing wisdom which could lead to criticism and rejection.[17] One of the authors of this book did research on the "Social Self and the Social Desirability Motive" and showed how our opinions are often influenced by social pressure.[18]

Another good example of witch-hunts and hysteria was the damage done to agriculture and apple production in the United States when an environmental group wrote a report linking Alar, an insecticide for apples, to health issues. This report was pushed by people who could profit from it.

Politicians didn't want to be seen as soft on matters vital to children's health. Alar was eventually taken off the market despite the fact that it was not harmful to children. This resulted in enormous financial losses to apple growers and U.S. agriculture in general.

If even 2% of Catholic Priests were involved in sex abuse, it's shameful and must be stopped. But as long as the Church buys property and raises money for charities, and some lawyers continue trolling for big bucks, the media will push new stories to the front page of newspapers and prime-time video and T.V. news. In a secular society, this may never end.

Chapter 18

President Hillary? Why we believe in checking out polls. Presidential polls predicted Hillary Clinton over Donald Trump and Thomas Dewey over Harry Truman. When should we question the polls? Can we rely on polls?

Recently, a newspaper criticized comments by the President of the United States because the information he used was from a poll with a small sample size. What they perhaps did not realize is that it is not the size of the sample, but how *representative* the sample is, that matters. The goal is to find people who really represent what we're inquiring about.

If you want to know the best strategy to use in a football game or the best football play to call under a certain set of circumstances, you could poll 10,000 football fans, carefully controlled according to age and background, or you could poll the top ten football coaches in America. Which poll do you think would give you the most valid results?

In many cases, polls can give us a realistic idea of what people are thinking or who is likely to win an election, but one must always be cautious about accepting what polls tell us. As we have seen in two major elections, the experts and the polls got it wrong in 2016 when they projected that Donald Trump would not be elected president and that the people of the United Kingdom would not vote to leave the European Union. The polls also were highly inaccurate in the French presidential primaries. How could the polls have been so wrong on such major and well-known issues?

Be careful of the pollsters, or at least the writers who create exciting headlines to promote newspapers, magazines, and on-line viewership. In August, 2016, a bold headline stated: WHITE CHRISTIAN AMERICA IS DYING. We think polls are often like the Rorschach Assessment Technique: You can see what you want to see in the ink blots. However, when we go to buy a car, we check the fine print on the contract. This is also a marvelous idea when analyzing polls.

The fine print in the above report says that White Christian America is a *metaphor* (an image or symbol) for the dominant culture built by white Protestants. So here the pollsters are really talking about Protestant America. In the very same paragraph the writer says "Catholics simply do not fit neatly into the story of White Christian America."[1]

Of course, we expect inaccuracy in casual polls that are meant to be entertaining and are not making an effort to be scientific or thorough. These are the types of polls that you find online or in fundraising solicitations. Political parties sometimes send out questionnaires asking our opinion on important topics, but they are only mailing these forms to people in their own political party, whose views they can already guess. They want us to believe our opinion counts and that our views will be implemented. Of course, they also want us to contribute money to help support the party!

However, errors can also be found in professional, scientific polls, the ones that are released with sample sizes and "margins of error" and other scientific-sounding words. Even if they try to be accurate, they can make errors in collecting and interpreting information. One such error is coming up with a sample that doesn't really represent most of the people studied. Another is simple bias. We will look at a couple of these types of errors after reviewing problems with casual polls.

Here's an example: A poll was conducted on a website that specialized in religious tolerance, but the results were meaningless because of the sample used.[2] The poll creators wanted to find out what religious and non-religious people thought about same-sex marriage and whether people thought they had relied on the will of God in making that determination. Their sample underrepresented Christians somewhat (53% of the respondents identified as Christians), but the larger concern was that a whopping 13% identified as Wiccan (a religion often referred to as Pagan Witchcraft).

Their sample was not representative of Americans in general or religious Americans. It is known as a "convenience sample" – a sample that is easily obtained but not likely to represent the overall group being studied. They used a self-selected sample of people who were interested in going to this website.

Similar issues can be found in most online polls. If ESPN, the sports network, had a poll about who should pay for a new stadium, you would find out what *some* sports fans (those who routinely go to this sports website and respond to polls) think about the issue, but not what *all* sports fans think, and certainly not all of the people of a particular community or region. Reporting that a "New Poll Shows 80% Favor Public Funding of Stadium" would be misleading. A more accurate headline would be: "New Poll of Sports Fans on ESPN Site Shows 80% Favor Public Funding of Stadium."

Consider the results of a poll studying chocolate milk: A survey conducted by the Innovation Center for U.S. Dairy made headlines by reporting that seven percent of Americans think that chocolate milk comes from brown cows.[3] Is this an accurate poll? Do that many people really think that brown cows make chocolate milk?

It is certainly a possibility. Seven percent of adults are mentally challenged. Many others may not have had a decent education. Of course, it is also possible that people gave that response for other reasons. Perhaps they weren't paying attention or thought that it would be fun to give an absurd answer. Even with serious polls, people may decide for any number of reasons that they do not want to reveal their actual beliefs.

In the case of the 2016 U.S. presidential election, some voters apparently did not want to share their true beliefs in polls leading up to the election.[4] A possible explanation for this is found in the notion of "social desirability." Most people have a desire to please others in order to be seen as "normal" folks who share common values. Some may have been hesitant to tell a pollster that they would vote for Donald Trump because of the many negative images associated with Trump.

While the pollsters spent thousands of dollars trying to find a good representative sample and obtain accurate results, they got it wrong. That difference of a few percentage points, that social desirability may have created, was enough to change the predicted outcome of the election.[5]

The most famous case of polling errors in the U.S. goes back to the presidential election of 1948. Harry Truman won the election and remained president despite the polls predicting a big win for the challenger, Thomas Dewey. President Truman made this event memorable by holding up the Chicago Tribune newspaper whose headline stated: "Dewey Defeats Truman." What went wrong? Sampling bias may have been the culprit, as pollsters used names from telephone books and not everyone could afford a phone at that time.

PART SIX
Undressing the Devil

Beelzebub's apparel is big, bright, and stylish, but sometimes he likes to wear a white lab coat. His new pitchfork has two prongs: *science* and *media*.

Chapter 19

Humans Aren't So Special After All

$\cdot R$obots are us. We don't really have free will.

Psychological studies by Asch, Milgram, and Zimbardo support the notion that man does not have free will. There are over 80,000 references to these studies in scientific journals. They show that humans will go to absurd lengths to conform to others wishes, rather than depend on their own independent judgment.

How was their study carried out? Volunteer teachers administered what they believed to be severe shocks to volunteer learners in another room, whenever the learner made an error. A white-coated scientist urged the "teacher" to increase the voltage, despite crying and screaming coming from the other room. The results? Sixty-five percent of the teachers administered the maximum shock of 450 volts!

Treating subjects in this way is, of course, unethical, but other problems with the study eventually surfaced. Milgram seems to have fudged some of his work because the volunteer teachers refused to shock much more than reported, and more teachers realized that the learners were actually actors and there were no actual shocks. These problems didn't surface for some time because the study wasn't replicated (repeated by other independent researchers) which is always a no-no.[1]

Once again, man outsmarts the brilliant and clever researchers. Not as easy as working with animals, is it, doctors? How many college students abandoned the Church because of these faulty studies? Again, only the Lord knows.

- Religion? Who needs it? Psychological research concludes that man's violent nature has declined. People are too smart today for old wives' tales and religious superstitions. There's no need today for all this religious hocus-pocus. After all, it's the same old stuff we learned in kindergarten, for God's sake.

  Psychologist Steven Pinker concludes that man's violent nature has declined because of the shift from valuing souls to that of valuing lives, and an increase in man's intelligence.[1b]

Pinker is right about one thing. The world is getting better when it comes to poverty and medical care. Less than 10% of the world now live in extreme poverty.[1c] But religion must take credit for a culture that values mankind and shares the benefits of stable governments and scientific advances. That's a long way from the pre-Christian Romans who thought of people as animals and actually enjoyed the murder of humans as entertainment.

Unfortunately, there is no evidence that man's violent nature has declined because of advances in science. Mankind's flaws are on display everyday with school shootings and high murder rates. Morality has more of an impact on violence than intelligence, and our intelligence is unchanged. So far, science has done better with technical hardware than with understanding and nourishing the soul. It produces life-saving procedures—and bombs that can blow us to bits.

How well have the nonreligious behaved? Just in the past 100 years, atheist regimes, including communist Russia, communist China, and Nazi Germany, have been responsible for approximately 100 million deaths. Adolf Hitler hated religion and compared it to a disease. The Nazis believed the Catholic Church was its strongest opposition. The Nazis' were promoting the survival of the fittest, based on the scientific theory of evolution and the concept of The Superman.

Even some religious folks have fallen for this agnostic reasoning and believe that if they're leading a good life they may be on track to a blessed eternity. But if you're really interested in reaching that Promised Land, we think the most direct route is to follow the teachings of Jesus Christ. We believe that the pompous, those who feel they have it made, and those who are putting themselves first, will be last. Not all that much like kindergarten, is it?

There's also the question of what constitutes good. Many dictators, presidents, and even Church officials let pride and arrogance drive them. They may think what they are doing is right—but as it turns out, it's anything but.

Is there any scientific evidence that a higher truth can fuse individual wills into common aspirations and efforts? Ara Norenzayan, at the University of British Colombia, published research showing that people and cultures with moralizing gods tend to be more generous. The researchers surveyed 600 religious believers around the world and their generosity with money. The more that people considered their god(s) to be moralizing and punitive, the more generously they shared money with a stranger.[2]

- Putting lipstick on little boys is a good idea. Except for different voice boxes and upper body strength, men and women are two peas in a pod. There's nothing special about being a man or a woman. The fair thing is to treat everyone the same.

Virginia's Fairfax County Public School District recently (2018) stripped the phrase biological gender from its Family Life Curriculum, replacing it with "sex assigned at birth."[2b] Some school systems believe that gender is a state of mind, not a result of biology. While we support their reaching out to the small number of students who are struggling with their gender identity, Catholics in the pews believe gender is biological. And plenty of Church teachings and research support that belief.

We read an article recently in a London, England newspaper that reviewed a TV program titled "The Secret Life of Five Year Olds." This particular article focused on gender differences and at what age they are "fixed." It questioned whether boardroom behavior begins in nursery school.

The writer asserts that gender options should remain open for every child because biological differences between males and females are "modest." The picture accompanying the story shows a little girl applying bright red lipstick to the lips of a five-year-old boy, who is wearing fluffy, feminine clothing.

The picture is cute, no doubt, but is it necessary, and where is all of this going? The article's final paragraph states: "It's the old adage. You can't be what you can't see." What our five-year-olds are seeing has become all too painfully clear.[3]

So is there something painful about what these kids are seeing? Somehow, we missed that, unless they mean boys acting like boys and girls acting like girls. (Careful, we mustn't let stereotypes rule us!)

What the article really reveals is that gender differences at age five are pretty much what parents have always experienced in the majority of their kids. As with any generalization, there are always exceptions, but the TV show reported the following:

- The boys' football (soccer) team loses a penalty shootout and the angry captain says he is changing his team's name to "suckers". He then begins to sulk and blame his mates.

- When left to their own devices, boys trash the studio while the girls are more competent and compliant. Extra tasks need to be added to keep the girls busy.

- Boys are also blunt in their opinions and refer to a drink made by their teacher as disgusting, while the girls tactfully indicate it is good but admit they don't like certain flavors.

- What about so-called "gender fluidity?" When these five-year-old TV "actors" are asked to cross-dress, the boys are horrified. This is what the professionals interviewed for the article call "gender boundary maintenance." Most parents have other, less fancy names for this.

The writer of this article finally seeks professional input. In response, a psychologist states that our personalities are not fixed but are rather like plastic (referring here to the brain, we think), and it takes until the mid-20s to really complete maturity (of the brain).

So, does boardroom behavior really begin in nursery school? We think the answer is no. Boardroom behavior begins at conception, with powerful genetic influences, and is affected strongly, even in the first[12] months of life, as pointed out in neuropsychological research from the University of South Florida. After that, future behavior is influenced through early life, with solidification in the early 20s, but plenty of opportunities for changes in behavior, even after that.

What's the point of trying to show that gender differences are modest when they really aren't? Unfortunately, what isn't raised in this article is what we might lose if we do not have a firm gender identity. Is it good not to feel comfortable with one's own identity? What about a father as a role model for his son, or a daughter accepting her mother as a role model? Truth be told, males and females differ in so many ways that it would require an encyclopedic listing to cover even a small percentage of those differences.

Why then do we see continuing journalistic efforts to soften gender differences? Is this a response to the highly publicized but small percentage of people who express trans-gender feelings? Or does it go much deeper and reflect a longing to know where we came from, how our personalities develop, and where we are headed as humans?

Before we go too far, we had better question the ethics of exposing a general population of children to this type of exploratory research on gender identity. We hope that most research granting agencies would have concern about enticing kids to forego their biological sex-role predisposition in order to study what happens in their lives over the following 25 years. What are the unknown and negative effects of experimenting with kids' sexual identity?

If we ask the casual observer on the street, we find that most people believe the genders differ in their behavior and emotions, and of course these differences go back to the brain. Standup comedians love the humor involved in pointing out these differences. Some joke that men compartmentalize their thoughts and have one box for each subject such as wife, children, car, sex, (and mother-in-law in the basement!). And the boxes must never touch each other.

Another much talked about difference is navigation. People have observed that most men don't ask for directions while women do, and that women navigate by relying on maps or local signposts such as "take a right after the McDonald's," while men claim to have big maps in their heads.

One popular explanation for these supposed brain differences is the division of labor experienced by our Hunter – Gatherer ancestors. Men needed to range widely in order to trap and kill animals (Tarzan?) and would run through the bush triangulating their position relative to fast-moving prey. They also had to react quickly, perhaps impulsively, to defend against attack. This might explain why more males suffer from attention deficit disorder.

Women, on the other hand, cultivated food and learned to verbally communicate with others to fend off male aggression, sexual and otherwise. This need to feel a sense of belonging in a social group is called need for affiliation. Our common sense and science tell us that women in general are more inclined to build relationships in a social group. Most men need and enjoy affiliation, but to a lesser extent than women.[4]

Those supporting the equality of male and female brains are suspicious of Hunter-Gatherer historical reports or believe they're not relevant today. After all, common sense told us the earth was flat and the sun rotated around our planet.

We believe they are still relevant. It's been known for some time that the male brain operates at the extremes. Males have more speech problems, attention-deficit disorders, and intellectual challenges in general. Males have also made up most of the truly gifted such as Einstein and Mozart. Women are more balanced. The male brain also matures more slowly, including the critical frontal lobe, the "orchestra leader" that ties together all the different areas of the brain. If you don't believe us, check out auto insurance policy rates for sixteen-year-old boys versus girls.

A funny thing happened on the way to Buckingham Palace: The authors established the first full-day school in England for kids with learning disabilities and attention-deficit disorder. Naturally, most of the students were boys. One day, the government showed up and threatened to close us down. Why? We didn't have 50% boys and 50% girls, as prescribed by English laws that protect against discrimination. With some help from the U.S. Embassy and a chance visit by the First Lady of the United States, along with a paid British consultant, we managed to squeak through this bureaucratic obstacle. The Brits continued to worry about this puzzling disregard for their man-made rules, but, we're sorry, the brain comes from God, not us.

There are a staggering number of connections and chemical interactions in the brain. It is made up of 100 billion neurons and a quadrillion synaptic connections (a message linking one part of the brain with another part of the brain). Even more limiting to our research is the fact that the brain is trying to study itself, and all of us, scientists and non-scientists, have biases that have developed out of our experiences. These experiences can also influence how we interpret scientific findings.

If there are real differences between the genders, they should show up in studies of animals. And they do. Here is a quick review. In guinea pigs, male aggression is due to prenatal masculinization of the brain. Also, male primates are more aggressive than female primates, while female primates are more *affiliative* (inborn need to belong to social groups) and more involved in social grooming and interacting with infants. Male adult rhesus monkeys are far more interested in playing with masculine human toys, i.e. wheeled toys, than feminine ones, i.e. stuffed animals; females prefer feminine toys.

Of course, hormonal differences affect the brain. Males are more rough-and-tumble even when testosterone levels are suppressed at birth. When pregnant monkeys are treated with testosterone their female offspring are more rough-and-tumble and aggressive than those not treated.

It's also possible to look at humans because of CAH, which is Congenital Adrenal Hyperplasia, a condition where the adrenal glands produce testosterone. CAH girls are more rough-and-tumble, play with masculine toys, and show less tenderness. CAH males are more aggressive, have better math scores, and are more assertive. They also suffer from a higher percentage of attention deficit disorder and autism.

An inverse of CAH is AIS, Androgen Insensitivity Syndrome, which results in insensitivity to testosterone. Women with AIS have less autism, are more anorexic, and have less athletic ability.

Those who do not support gender differences point out that the brain allows for plasticity, and some changes in the brain can take place based upon the environment and perhaps the culture in general. Maternal malnutrition impairs the fetal brain. Maternal stress leads to more substance abuse, poor diet, blood pressure, and poor immune defenses. And good rat mothering can even alter gene regulation.[5]

On average, men and women do differ with respect to brain and behavior changes. We believe the research shows these gender differences are more biological than environmental.

How much do social factors contribute to gender differences? The environment always plays a role in human development, but biological factors are critical when it comes to gender. When and if all social factors are neutralized in our society, we'll have an opportunity to really study the impact of biology. This is unlikely to happen because most people enjoy gender differences and tend to exaggerate them.[6]

A recent study by Daphna Joel of Tel Aviv University says the real question is exactly how different behaviors emerge. On average, men and women do differ with respect to some brain and behavior changes, but these differences are found in large numbers and cannot always be relied upon to predict individual behavior or attitudes.[7]

So where does all this leave us? We draw two conclusions. One is that there are differences between the genders, but when it comes to individual assessment one needs to look at behavior rather than theorizing about gender. This reliance on studying behavior is why the field of psychology has made progress over the past forty years. The study of behavior is much more reliable and achievable than guessing about what goes on inside a person's brain.

Our second conclusion has to do with arrogance. We still have a lot more to learn about the brain. We're reminded of a three-year-old at the beach filling her pail with water in an effort to diminish the size of the ocean, or to discover what is lurking at the bottom of the sea. We now have exploratory submarines and underwater research gear, but we should be careful about inferences about the brain and gender, although findings to date have been interesting.

Would we ever use perceptions about gender, based on research and experience, in decision making? We would need to conjure up an artificial situation such as being assigned to select 1000 individuals for hand-to-hand military combat, and the choice would be 1000 randomly-selected males or 1000 randomly-selected females. Based upon what we think we know, it would be foolish not to choose the males. While all the females could be better than all of the males at lugging 50 pound backpacks up steep mountain trails and engaging in guerrilla warfare, we think this is doubtful. However, there is no doubt that some of females would do better than some of the males. Marine Corp records show that, overall, female combat Marines can't keep up with males, and physical standards have been lowered to accommodate females.

When evaluating folks in the real world, on an individual basis, for occupations such as childcare or military combat, the best predictor of future behavior is past behavior, motivation, and rigorous evaluation—not gender.

- Do your own thing! Religion is full of up-tight control freaks. The church is so negative, always keeping us down and telling us what not to do.

Our society often suggests that inhibiting ourselves is not a good thing. Holding back on our behavior and feelings is not only old-fashioned, but can lead to anxiety and perhaps even (God forbid) neurosis! You gotta' be free, right? Isn't our country all about freedom?

While disclosing our private, inner feelings to trusted friends and family members is healthy, holding back on behavior and even feelings is helpful in adjusting to life. Someone once said "it takes a village," and regulating certain behaviors and feelings is necessary for family and community.

Humans are the most out of control at the age of two. "The defiant twos." We've seen plenty of parents who've had out-of-control children in that time frame. That's why we always emphasized structure as well as love. On the other hand, it's easy to blame parents when they have a truly oppositional child. Professional help is sometimes necessary. Children never become truly free if they can't learn self-control. Even dogs need to be socialized and we're a lot more complex than dogs.[8]

The Church has always shaped our society, law, and culture, by pointing out higher truths that allow us to work together. And these moral commands have an *inhibiting* effect on our behavior. We don't always like this, but—to paraphrase Sigmund Freud—'inhibition is the price of civilization'.[9]

It's good to remember that a crossing guard is not there to prevent us from crossing the street: rather, the guard guides us and keeps us safe. Because of the guard's efforts, and the laws developed for the overall good of the community that underlie his or her job, we more quickly and safely reach our destination.

Being a Catholic does require a bit of "true grit," though. We have lots of do's and don'ts, along with the expectation that we will attend Mass on Sundays, sacrifice goodies like yummy chocolate candy and accomplish extra works during the Lenten season. We believe these rituals and rules give us additional structure—and we are in plenty need of that.

Some Protestant denominations may be easier to follow. In fact, Karl Marx once stated that Protestantism was "the last outpost on the way to atheism." We don't think Marx knew much about religion, and certainly our Southern Baptist friends and other Protestant denominations here in Florida have stood with us for Christian behavior and against the culture of death.[10]

The idea of unfettered freedom is a normal human desire. One of the authors had the privilege of receiving clinical training at the University of Wisconsin in Madison where famed psychologist, Harry Harlow, was conducting research on motivation. He gave hungry monkeys a choice between opening a door to obtain food and opening a door to view a toy train charging around a circular railway track. If you think those monkeys took the food, you're wrong. Curiosity and motivation are, indeed, basic drives.[11] (Hey, maybe there really is something to this evolution idea, after all)!

But sometimes too much freedom at an early age leads to emotional problems or drug abuse. The outcome is usually not good. We are reminded of the movie Thelma and Louise. While this Hollywood classic won Academy Awards and showcased good acting, we can't recommend it because of the culture of death lifestyle "enjoyed" by the protagonists. Drugs, free sex, theft, brutality, and dishonesty, gave it an R rating, which, of course, ensured that a lot of folks would watch it. Our heroines end it all by driving their shiny new Cadillac convertible off the edge of the Grand Canyon.

This dramatic and spectacular ending seems like a fist in the face to people in the pews who try to lead balanced lives. It was a Hollywood stand for freedom, but it must've hurt like heck when the car hit the rocks 2000 feet below! Maybe it's a good idea to avoid the rocks, even if that means developing a bit of self-control.

Chapter 20

Religion Has Always Kept Science Down

Not only did Christianity make science possible, but there are many Catholics, including Catholic theologians, who are scientists. The theologian and mathematician Marin Mersenne studied celestial mechanics.[1] Matteo Ricci used scientific explanations to teach church doctrine in China.[2] In modern times, a Catholic priest, Father Georges Lemaître, proposed the *Big Bang Theory* that supports Christian teachings.[3]

Our Catholic catechism tells us that questions about the origins of the world and of man have been the object of many scientific studies and "these discoveries invite us to even greater admiration for the greatness of the Creator."[4]

If it were not for Christianity, there would have been little science as we know it today. Unlike previous religions and philosophies, we Christians believe God doesn't micromanage every event in our complex world but instead gives us freedom to explore and discover some things for ourselves.

American Jesuit brother, Guy Consolmagno, the pope's chief astronomer and an MIT graduate, stated that once his scientist friends realized he was a Jesuit they started telling him about the churches they went to.[4b] We don't think you'll hear much about this from our secular friends in the media.

Prior to Christianity, Romans and citizens of some other nations believed in many different gods. Gods of fire, gods of love, and gods of power, to name just a few, depending on a person's own desires and preferences. Everyone had their favorites, and these gods were totally unpredictable. They might be fighting with other gods or show up at any time or place—without an invitation.

This helter-skelter world made science impossible. Christianity believes in one God who created the earth and who set things in motion in an orderly fashion. Christians carried this message to the entire world. Belief in one God was necessary to have reliability. Any scientist will tell you that research cannot be true or valid unless it is first reliable.

If you were a scientist who created a new spelling test in which the same people retook the test on several occasions, without additional instruction, and had widely differing scores, your test would not be reliable and therefore could not be valid. That's why scientists invest enormous effort to control all outside factors that could inadvertently influence their research.

A research psychologist at a leading university used rats in an investigation of motivation. Her findings seemed valid until they were replicated (repeated) at another university. The results just didn't hold up. After thinking this through, the scientist realized she had unknowingly made "pets" of some of the rodents by giving them cute names and holding and stroking them. This affected the research and made it unreliable. So after controlling for a wide variety of factors that could interfere with a perfect piece of research, these friendly touches interfered with reliability, which in turn crippled the research design and the results.[5]

Sometimes secular research appears on the surface to downplay religion. For example, Andrew Newberg studied Tibetan Buddhist monks, cloistered nuns, and Pentecostals who spoke in tongues. Using radioactive isotopes, he found that the nuns and monks showed excitation in some parts of the brain and had shut down other parts.[6]

Some secularists are eager to jump on these kinds of findings and say there is nothing special about human morality and human potential. "They are just hardwired products of evolution." But we need to be careful or we can misunderstand scientific studies such as Newberg's.

The misunderstanding often comes from cause and effect. What starts something versus what's the result of something? Everything we say or do lights up the message boards of our brain, but that doesn't mean those different parts of the brain *cause* us to have religious feelings. It just means the feelings register somewhere in the brain, with concentration and meditation changing which parts of the brain are used to focus on these feelings.

This is an example of questionable interpretation of findings. Earlier, we reviewed various obstacles to good research. Even when scientists use impeccable and rigorous methods leading to accurate research, the *interpretation* of the findings can still lead us astray.

• Christians aren't too smart. Professors aren't all that religious. Have you noticed?

It's true that some college professors are not religious. Aren't these about the smartest people around? Maybe so, when it comes to abstract academics, but not necessarily when it comes to common sense and realistic judgements about life. Maybe we have to question whether college is the best place to learn about the real world. Fewer than 25% of the entire United States population complete college in four years.

When Pope John Paul visited his native Poland in 1979, "millions of people took to the street, to the horror of the *college educated* communist regime, chanting 'we want God'."[7] (Authors' emphasis)

It's true that some intellectuals don't support Christianity. The same thing was true at the time of Christ. Educators get caught up in their own culture and don't want to be out of step with their peer group, much as is the case with any teenager, young adult, or adult. Nevertheless, many intellectuals do privately profess a belief in God. Vanity and egos play a part, as well.

Some of the brightest individuals throughout the centuries have been Christian theologians. In 2015, the United States Supreme Court was comprised of six justices who were Catholic and three who were Jewish. It's good to remember that Supreme Court decisions require practical wisdom as well as book learning.

Even if Catholics are no more intellectual than others, this in no way puts them outside the Christian view of salvation. Here are the words of Father Robert Persons, who wrote *The Christian Directory* in *1582* (Yes, that's 1582; not 1982):

"Nether, when he had to make a kyng first in Israell, did he seeke owt the ancientest blood, but tooke Saul, of the basest tribe of Jews, and after him, David the poorest sheephearde of all his brethren. And when he came into the world, he soght not owt the noblest men to make princes of the earth, that is, to make Apostles, but tooke of the poorest, and simplest, thereby to confound, (as one of them sayeth), the foolish vanitie of this world in making so great account of the preeminence of a little fleshe and bloode in this lyfe.[8]

- Sex is sport and women have missed out.

Yes, women in years past missed out on lots of things that are more available to them today, such as depression, sexually transmitted diseases, and the guilt of abortion. On the other hand, they had societal support for stable marriages, wonderful families, the joy of child rearing, just plain respect, and the sense of meaningfulness in God's plan. Hookup behavior in our secular society tends to play down negatives stemming from unrestrained sexual behaviors and even promote them as "cool," but the results of these choices also include physical illnesses such as syphilis, gonorrhea and other infections. Not so cool then.

When and how did sex become sport for some women? Well, there was "the pill," which reduced some of the fear of pregnancy, though not for men if the woman decided not to take the pill or just forgot. And there have been cases where a woman hopes for pregnancy because she thinks the man is a "keeper" or he can be leveraged for big bucks through a paternity suit. Sadly, men and women are equally adept at manipulation.

This new attitude was aided by the Kinsey Report at the University of Indiana. Its results were interpreted to mean that women had strong sexual desires that they had denied because of cultural attitudes. But that research was somewhat suspect because of the subjects in the study. If there was religious and cultural shame attached to sexual sport for woman—and there was—where did they find these willing subjects and were they representative of most women? Probably not, as there may have been a "self-selection" bias.

But the results of the study supported the idea that women had intense sexual desires, similar to those of a man.

We think some of this shift in morality came from the negative side of the Feminist movement. Not the positive side that encourages women to better understand and achieve their callings and abilities, but the negative side that insists men and women are the same and that woman need to duplicate men's attitudes and behaviors. We wonder, do professors who advise female students to happily hook up, pay for anti-depressants and other meds?

Research shows that women's hookup behavior in college is correlated with significant depressive symptoms.[9] Studies show that teenagers who engage in casual sex are more likely to suffer from depression than peers who do not engage in casual sex. Teens who don't engage in sex were rated lowest for clinical depression.[10] Depression and suicide rates are much higher now than in the 1950s.

Let's turn to a non-scientific source that relies on common sense and spiritual input. We are referring to the Torah, as interpreted by Dennis Prager in his book, *The Rational Bible*.[10b] Prager is a biblical scholar and radio personality. We believe the Old Testament was inspired by God, but its tenets have become common sense for many of us, because we've been accepting and following them for a long, long, time.

In Prager's opinion, Western society underwent the sexual revolution after World War II, with the weakening of biblical values and the ease of obtaining contraception and abortion. In addition to creating more fatherless children than ever before, this revolution has harmed both sexes, especially women.

Men have also suffered, Prager says, because fewer men seek to marry and men benefit enormously from marriage. In addition, many men are less motivated to succeed in life, because in the past they did that to earn the commitment of a woman.

Let's hope and pray that men and women wake up. But meanwhile, thanks to the healing sacraments of the Church, especially the sacrament of reconciliation (confession), sincere individuals can be forgiven of their sins, no matter what they are or how great they are.

- Mothers aren't so special. Good food and daycare should do it. Women need to work to put food on the table—and a second car?

We know that mothers are special, but the research hasn't always been available. A limitation to good research is the pressure to withhold or alter findings in order to support whatever is politically popular at the time. For example, in the early days of women entering the marketplace, daycare centers were relied upon to provide child-rearing services. The authors can remember when *The Psychological Monitor*, a newspaper written by the American Psychological Association, published an article admitting that some professional journals had not accepted research showing the negative effects of daycare. They feared a firestorm of criticism.[11]

More recently, now that the "political heat is off," research has finally surfaced showing what's wrong with too much daycare or poorly operated daycare centers. Twenty-six percent of children who spend over 45 hours per week in daycare centers develop serious behavioral problems in school. This compares with 10% of children with less exposure to daycare.[11] Of course, the government isn't about to offer research grants for politically incorrect proposals, so these findings remain largely hidden.

So maternal child-rearing is important. On one popular street in Tampa Bay, Florida, we see mothers pushing beautiful, lace-trimmed baby carriages, but inside we find one or two, nicely dressed, and thoroughly spoiled, dogs! These moms are forsaking children for animals.

Yes, we do adore our pets, but they are not human beings created in God's image. People carry pets on airplanes for emotional support, but aren't the grown-ups there to provide emotional support to their human children? If they do that, maybe the kids will provide the emotional support their parents need when they grow old.

Why don't the fathers just raise the kids? Some can do it but we know child-rearing is a natural genetic predisposition and inclination for women. In Sweden, in 2018, either gender can take leave from work when children are born. The vast majority of workers taking that option are women.

At one time, "experts" believed kids in hospitals for extended times shouldn't have their mothers around. Better to give sick kids an antiseptic environment. What happened? The kids wasted away and died! One of the authors of this book saw children who had been locked up and ignored. It was pathetic and criminal—and sinful.

Trading family love and togetherness for a job and a car is a poor choice for humans in our world. With longer life-spans, we should be able to do both.

Harry Harlow, at the University of Wisconsin raised infant Rhesus monkeys with two artificial, pretend moms. One had a bottle of milk coming from its torso, while the other one had a terrycloth robe that simulated the mother monkey's fur. Guess which one the infant monkeys preferred?[12] The robe, of course. Yes, love over milk, love over food, love over busy schedules, love over daycare, and love over carpooling. Need we say more?

PART SEVEN

Inoculation, Why Do We Need It? "God is Dead," Gay Marriage, Abortion.

Chapter 21

Questions and Answers

"Stars have been hitting the red carpet all season long in sheer dresses that leave little to the imagination and offer a glimpse of their undergarments. Some of the hottest stars from Jenna Dewan Tatum to Ellie Goulding to Natalie Portman have shown off their skivvies in super-hot dresses that embrace this barely-there trend."[1]

Here's a quote from another catchy little magazine article: "You're thirsty and you've come to the right place, she purrs into the microphone, her voice husky and seductive. Here, the water flows eternally; here the party seems to go on forever."[2]

Man, how cool can you get? We'd all like seduction and eternal flow—just let it happen—but we're probably not going to find it in Times Square, New York City, U.S.A. (Not even Vegas?). Ha. No, the true road to paradise isn't so easy but is ever more joyful, and maybe even, gads! More fun.

Drip, drip, drip. In the United States, some newspapers and magazines continued to proclaim that, to be progressive, we must embrace new ways of thinking and feeling, denouncing traditional values. It isn't just an occasional essay, movie, or tweet. It used to be a slow drip, drip, drip, like water on a rock that gradually wore us down, but now we're getting a constant barrage of anti-traditional and anti-religious comments and stories. And so it goes, on and on, day after day.

A book for young children is endorsed by Occupy Wall Street.[3] Each illustrated page covers a letter of the alphabet: "C is for co-op, cooperating cultures—creative counter to corporate vultures!"

"Megaphones marching, it must be May Day." "Radical Reds!" Rabble rousing Riff Raff." Really?" (Illustration showing Martin Luther King and a priest in Roman collar in a peaceful, candle-lit procession).

"W is for workers' rights. X is for Malcolm as in Malcolm X. Remember Parks, remember King, and remember Malcolm—and let freedom ring! The letter Z is for Zapatista, of course" *(Leader of a revolutionary leftist political and militant group).*

To properly defend ourselves and our Church from all this nonsense, we'd like to offer inoculations similar to those designed to protect us from diseases such as: pneumonia, chickenpox, and influenza. This inoculation will prepare our minds for worldly criticism. These challenges may come from family, friends, or work associates. Jesus warned us that maintaining our faith would not be easy.

Hopefully, a question-and-answer format will make this inoculation less painful. So hold on, the needle will only sting for a few seconds. These questions come from the authors of this book or from people that they know. Let's try a few:

What is the criticism you as a Christian will encounter the most; the one you will have most difficulty dealing with? What could be so painful? What could be so dangerous?

Our answer:—silence.

Yes, silence. In a secular society most folks just ignore religion in their day to day conversations. They may explore issues such as politics, education, or even dying, and never bring up God or religion. When people don't talk about something, it's a little like saying it doesn't exist—or at least it's not important. When is the last time your friends said a prayerful thanksgiving before dining?

If your beliefs go unnoticed and are pushed into the background, what does that mean? What does that make you, an outsider? Are you someone who is old-fashioned, superstitious, and out of touch with what is cool and vibrant today? Being a Catholic is a little like being on the outer fringe of our popular culture. When agnostics and even other Christians learn you're a Catholic, you'll sometimes notice a reflexive look of puzzlement, as though you're an uneducated hillbilly or a member of the Flat Earth Society.

Why organized religion? Protestants talk a lot a lot about an individual relationship with Jesus; no popes, bishops, or priests necessary. It's kind of like the Outback Steakhouse slogan: "no rules; just right." Organized religion simply creates a bureaucracy that gets in the way; I'll do it all by myself.

Sometimes it does get in the way, but it also gives us the structure and support we've needed to survive 2000 years. Our line of bishops and priests, under one pope, goes back to the first century. Jesus seemed to prefer group services and said something along the lines of: "Whenever three or more are gathered in my name, I will be with them." We authors have this old-fashioned motto: "God knows best."

Some people who claim to be Catholic set their own rules and accept only the doctrines of the Church they agree with. We call them "Cafeteria Catholics." Unfortunately, many of them go directly to the cafeteria dessert table and sometimes don't even pay their full share of the bill. This is one of the ways martyrs helped the early church: "This is tough going. No free rides here."

We authors spoke with an artist who said she was spiritual but didn't need religion. She didn't want rules and doctrines. "They are cold and formal. Too many rules," she said. And, anyway, she was already "warm and caring" and wanted to "save the environment." She said that she relied on the Bible until she found some words of encouragement, needing nothing more than the Bible.

In a very gentle sort of way we told her about William James, the psychologist and philosopher, who said some folks think they know God but they are just projecting what they think is right and fair onto this entity they call God. We asked her to think about this because she might be reflecting ideas she learned from her culture rather than what God really wants. She might be creating her own "god" rather than following inspired writings that tell us who God is and what's on *his* agenda—not ours.

We also pointed out that St. Paul makes it clear that tradition is necessary. St. Paul's preaching was accepted as the word of God and this was before the New Testament had been written. The Catholic Church is the storehouse of that tradition.[4]

Friedrich Nietzsche was a brilliant philosopher, and he didn't believe in God.

A key figure in the "God is Dead" movement was Friedrich Nietzsche, who was born in 1844 and became a close friend of the famous operatic symphonist, Richard Wagner. In Nietzsche's classic book, *Thus Spoke Zarathustra,* he developed the theme, of the Superman. He believed that he was "entirely body and nothing more, and the soul is only the name of something in the body."[5]

Nietzsche's work probably influenced Adolf Hitler, who picked up on this theme. Nietzsche suffered brain dementia from syphilis and died of a heart attack at the age of 44, while under the care of his sister. When his sister died, Adolf Hitler attended her funeral.

Some agnostic neuropsychologists share Nietzsche's viewpoint because they can't seem to find a soul hiding inside the brain, which is a silly quest when you think about it—and they don't seem to be looking that hard!

Atheists make up less than 5% of the American population, but some are energetic and emotional, "evangelists" for their own philosophy of life. Most of them see little value in the "mythology" of religion and would be happy to see the concept disappear.

Naturally, we don't agree with atheists. We believe it's they who are unrealistic. They believe religion encourages the idea that humans are weak and fragile, thus making them dependent on religion. Science, however, has clearly demonstrated that we are, indeed, a very fragile lot, an extremely fragile lot.

During the first 12 months of life, the brain will experience more changes than at any other time in its life span. If we suffer physical or emotional abuse, our brain will not develop properly. Neuropsychologists at the University of South Florida, St. Petersburg, report that just having a mother suddenly change her facial expression from one of love and sympathy to a frowning scowl sends the infant brain into destructive spasms that can be measured on an MRI (brain imaging machine).[6]

Many of the atheists we have met are rather smug folks who are convinced of their own intellectual superiority. They don't feel the need to depend on others and one of their "Bibles" is Ayn Rand's book, *Atlas Shrugged*. Rand was an atheist who emphasized individualism and high aspirations. Her characters don't believe in self-sacrifice for the sake of others and the supernatural is an unnecessary delusion. We agree that *Atlas Shrugged* is an interesting book that makes valid points and have enjoyed Rand's other works.

There are, however, problems with her colorful characters. They are self-starters who don't seem to need structure or authority in their lives. To operate as successfully as they do, they would need very high IQs, probably falling in the top 2%. What's to be done with the other 98% of the population? And who raised these superheroes of business and architecture? Did they just appear fully grown, without help from parents, community, or religious values? We don't think so.

Catholic Church political views actually support part of Rand's concept. We believe in starting at the lowest, most independent level (subsidiarity), with the individual and family, then expanding to the community and the state, when necessary. This concept includes free markets and profit-making. So far so good. But Catholics also believe in solidarity and human dignity. So we believe it's important to watch out for each other and not just focus on the enrichment of the self. We support social security and safety nets.

Here's an observation that sums up our position: "Sneering at religion is simply lazy thinking. Sooner or later it dawns on us that life has meaning, and if we look at the accumulated bank of maybe 30 million years of human knowledge, it becomes clear that this evidence is radically limited. We don't know where we came from, where we are going, and why we are here."[7]

Atheists may lack empathy because they are unrealistic about themselves and others. Is this why their wondrous logic didn't lead them to end slavery? They probably didn't notice the slaves since their self-direction doesn't include most other people, let alone uneducated minorities.

Ask your atheist acquaintances how much they give to charity and how many volunteer hours they commit. They have no rational basis for morality. The low per capita giving of American atheists to charities is not surprising.

A study by Harvard University professor Robert Putnam found that religious people are more charitable than their irreligious counterparts. Some 40% of worship service-attending Americans volunteer regularly to help the poor and elderly as opposed to 15% of Americans who never attend services. Religious individuals are also more likely to volunteer for school and youth programs (36% versus 15%), neighborhood or civic groups (26% versus 13%), and for healthcare (21% versus the 13%).[8]

We discuss our Church's incredible record of charitable giving elsewhere in the book, but Peter J. Rubinstein gives us a great example of Judeo-Christian generosity. Rubinstein's grandfather, who was a poor tailor in New York, borrowed money every Friday afternoon to fulfill the commandment of giving tzedakah before the Jewish Sabbath. He then repaid his debt the following week, once he had some money. Amazing! Rubinstein asserts: "Generosity is at the heart of Christianity, Islam and Judaism."[9]

Effective living is a mixture of spirituality, creativity, and self-control. The importance of self-control is confirmed scientifically by Roy F. Baumeister's research at Florida State University, which we used to illustrate our research on the early Church.[10]

In fact, self-control is one of the most important ingredients necessary for academic and occupational success. We authors can confirm these finding based on our years of experience as therapists. Lack of conscious self-control can lead to guilt, depression, and devastating moral and secular outcomes.

Isn't the Catholic Church out of step with modern times? For example, many Protestant denominations have accepted married clergy, women priests, artificial birth control, gay marriage, and abortion.

Yes, we are. We're way out of line—isn't it great? Sometimes it's a good idea to be out of step with rapidly changing modern cultures. It also helps us to avoid watered-down Christianity such as that found in the 2016 movie version of *Ben-Hur*. According to Charlotte Allen, most of the Messiah's comments were just a mix of popular but worn out phrases about peace and forgiveness rather than offering a complete understanding of Christianity's demands and rewards."[11]

Regarding married clergy and women priests, the Church uses Christ as its model for the highest good. Some might argue, and with good reason, that the culture at the time of Christ would not permit women to have such a lofty status. The Church's position is that Christ, as God, selected the time in history to make his earthly appearance and knew full well what he was doing. Married Episcopal priests, who join the Catholic Church, can remain married, but ordination into the Catholic priesthood, following the model of Christ, requires full sacrifice and dedication to God, the Church, and its mission.

Women are important in the Catholic Church; no one reveres Mary, the mother of Jesus, more than we do. And Mary Magdalene was the only person to directly observe the death of Jesus on the cross and discover that his body was no longer in the tomb. The saintly Thomas Aquinas called Mary Magdalene the "apostle of the apostles."[12] This book is written for people in the pews, and it was the people in the pews who demanded greater veneration for Mary.

Why is the church against homosexuals? Gay people are just born that way. God must've wanted them or they wouldn't be here.

That's a very good question. We don't know if there is any special mission or significance to be found in homosexuality. The authors have evaluated priesthood candidates for the past 35 years and the Church has never told us that gays can't be priests. The fact that the Church is willing to accept gays as priests tells us something about its real-life position on this issue. Once again, while the church shows love and mercy toward individual gay persons, we're back to institutional decisions about what is best for all Catholics.

Pope Benedict XVI indicated in his book, Light of the World, that homosexuals are "human beings with their own problems and joys. They deserve respect and should not be discriminated against." At the same time, Pope Benedict points out that the true meaning and direction of sexuality is to bring about the union of a man and a woman.[13]

Where does this leave the average Catholic homosexual? Here's a statement from a gay Catholic: "I agree totally with the Church's teaching that sex must be open to life, but I would suggest that if I and another man come together in intimacy and mutual non-exploitative love, that union is open to life. There is nothing more life-changing and indeed life creating than the experience of deep unconditional love.

"I believe the perfect template for this is the Mass. It is a time when a sometimes disordered and unruly group of people, with all their hang-ups and brokenness, living in their isolated worlds, gather together and through the power of the Holy Spirit and his love become one body which is open to and creates new life."[14]

Once again we have institutional decisions and judgments based on what, in the Church's universal judgment, is best for humankind as a whole. These judgments aren't always easy to bear when one views individual cases in the day-to-day world, especially the world of secularism and the culture of death.

The pope called for a year of mercy in 2016, and all of us can be forgiven, regardless of our trespasses. At the same time, the Church is firm in its pronouncements that marriage be open to life, both socially and sexually. In fact, this steadfast attitude, which is not based on popularity or current trends, is a defining virtue that attracts people to the Church.

Natural birth control? The "rhythm method?" Nobody practices it.

Some people do, but this is a tricky question, especially in our financially well-off culture, because married people naturally want to exert control in order to plan a family, rather than just letting a family happen. Many criticize Pope Paul VI and his *Humanae Vitae* for banning artificial birth control.

Most American Catholics believe their use of artificial birth control for family planning is not morally wrong, but here again we need to remember that, unlike other earthly institutions, the church does not rely on popularity polls to determine its moral judgments.[15] Some folks believe the major thrust of Pope Paul's encyclical was more about a contraceptive society and the culture of death and less about contraception per se, but that could be a cop out.[16]

In recognizing that artificial birth control teachings as an institution offers a slippery slope to large-scale abortion and the culture of death, Pope Paul was right on target. In our view, any pope's writings should reflect what is best for society as a whole. Most Catholics don't realize that the church could endorse artificial birth control in a developing country, for example, if it was necessary and less of an evil than say loss of spiritual freedom or the certain destruction of the people.

Also, Natural Family Planning is taught by the Church as a very respectful and even *feminist* approach to birth control. While the "rhythm method" is frequently ridiculed in secular culture, Natural Family Planning is a scientific approach that is highly effective, teaches women (and men) to better understand reproduction, and does not rely on the ingestion of drugs or hormones. Unlike artificial birth control, it is a truly natural approach that places responsibility on both the man and the woman.

Abortion has nothing to do with killing a child, because a fetus is not really a human until it is older and takes on the shape of a child.

Really? Here are some words of wisdom from a British clinical neuroscientist, Neil Scolding: "When does the developing fetus acquire the moral status of a live human is a non-question, the answer being so self-evident. It must do so when it becomes a live human, and it is a live human from its very beginning. Human is a species—in the embryo of which we speak—and at any time in its development is a member of no other."

Scolding points out that moral status shouldn't depend on size. He separates the notion of being a human from the notion of personhood. Personhood comes later, but humanness is there from its very beginning.[17] The unborn child is alive because the child's body takes in nutrients that allow it to survive and the unborn child's heart tends to beat about three weeks after conception.[18]

While most people dislike the notion of terminating human life, for many that feeling is secondary to their view of a mother's rights, career advancement, and other secular priorities. As Mary Cunningham Agee points out, there are four basic influences that weigh heavily in all abortion decisions: the fear that having the baby will cause the mother to lose her relationship with the baby's father, or her own family, or damage her social standing or career.[19]

Is the church's longevity really such a big deal? We know that scientific odds show its exceptionalism, but what do I tell my critical friends?

Yes, it's a huge deal. Here's what John Russell says: "What lasts? Aren't we all searching for things that last and sustain us? Since the time of Christ, many nations and rulers have come and gone; cities and cultures have thrived and passed away. There have been many calamities, revolutions, world wars, and natural disasters.

Many things on earth that people expected to last forever are no longer here. Yet, the Catholic Church has endured for more than 2,000 years, surviving controversy and scandal (crusades, excessive power in the Middle Ages, corruption, the recent sex abuse tragedies), and yet it continues to grow. This fact certainly enhances our faith when it gets shaky."[20]

Indeed, the papacy is the oldest continuously functioning institution in the world. If anyone wonders whether the papal story still matters, we can recall the death of Pope John Paul II. Over four million people streamed into Rome, and many people waited up to 30 hours to pay respects to John Paul.

Many people jostled for a place, including the Prince of Wales. Media outlets, all over the globe, devoted almost continuous coverage to the solemn events that marked the passing of one pontificate and the beginning of another. It stands as the biggest media event in history.[21]

176

Bet those four million people weren't the cream of high society! No Hollywood celebs, either.

You've got that right, my friend. A few were, but most weren't, thank God.

Doesn't it all boil down to just being good to others? I have friends who are just as nice as I am, maybe nicer, and I don't see them going to church.

Yes, true religion is necessary. The "religion of niceness" has its limitations. Smith and Denton investigated the religious life of American teenagers. It appears that for some of them, religion is just the experience of feeling good, happy, secure, and at peace. "For them, God is something like a combination divine butler and cosmic therapist, and is always on call to take care of any problem that arises."[22]

Here is a nice way of putting it: For Christians, Jesus is not simply a good man whose example we follow—he is our source and strength for everything we do. Our lives—no matter how good and well-intentioned—will not bear the fruit we desire unless we are rooted in Christ.[23]

Wouldn't you know it, science informs us that there's a link between church attendance and reported happiness: Eighty-six percent of church-goers report "satisfied" or "very satisfied lives."[24]

Getting back to having nice friends who don't attend church, Ross Douthat gives us his "cut flowers" explanation of why people can be nice without supporting religion, but why religion is still necessary. To paraphrase Douthat, today's nice people are the result of Judeo-Christian values which span several thousand years.

These responsible attitudes need to be taught, and your nice friends and their parents and grandparents, have been blessed by Judeo-Christian values. The nice people you refer to have cut the flowers from the plant of values and benefited. While this is good, if no one continues to plant the flowers and till the soil, there will be no flowers for future "nice people."[25] Numerous scientific findings help us, here again, by demonstrating that people aren't born with kind and loving attitudes.

What if I begin to feel "iffy" about not only my Catholic faith, but religion in general?

At some point most of us have doubts or difficulties about our spiritual beliefs and wishes. Could a Jew, living in a tiny outpost of the mighty Roman Empire, who held no great position in society and who was persecuted and eventually executed as a common criminal, really be God? Some people leave the church or stop attending services, but many return when they experience the ups and downs of life or wonder what our life means if there is no God. Knowledge and experience have a way of changing attitudes. Prayer doesn't hurt, either. Be patient and keep an open mind.

A good friend of mine believes that the story of Jesus Christ is just that—a great story, but fiction none-the-less.

Ok, why don't we go with your friend's theory? The story of Christ and his followers was a neat bit of storytelling and today might win a Pulitzer Prize; just beautifully and gloriously written fiction. It has become the most popular book of all time and its power is unquestioned. It has inspired hundreds of millions of people from all walks of life, so these writers must have had more talent than Shakespeare or any other contemporary writers. This was indeed writing of huge proportions.

If today's book publishers existed back then, would they have accepted it? Notwithstanding that Mathew, Mark, Luke and John didn't have a credentialed agent, their story is full of flaws.

Science-fiction wasn't in then; all of those miracles would be considered "over-the-top." Then, you have the hero of the story associating with tax collectors and prostitutes—in that time and culture?

Another editor might complain that women were said to be eyewitnesses to the resurrection, but their low social status wouldn't even allow them to testify in court. Most editors would put all of this down to lazy writing and advise the author—or in this case, the team of authors—to get their act together and come down to earth.

Who were these authors? Did they write other books, and how well did they sell? Did these fishermen and agricultural workers take a quickie online course in fiction-writing to come up with this tale? One of them, Luke, was a physician, and then there was that Roman citizen Saul (Paul). Luke was close to St. Paul, but neither of them knew Christ personally.

What was their publication platform? Did they have a syndicated TV audience or a few hundred thousand followers on Facebook and Twitter? How would these unknowns get the word out? And who would buy it? Well, no, the whole thing just didn't add up.

The editors might then have switched gears and started to wonder whether this so-called "fiction" was based on something that really happened! Were these literary imposters trying to take credit for something they actually witnessed? There could be no other explanation. In any event, in the opinion of the editorial board, this attempt at fiction wouldn't sell and wouldn't be worth the time, effort, and money needed to promote it.

Okay, so the Christian story may not be fiction, but wasn't Jesus just a Holy Prophet and nothing more?

Mohammed respected the teachings of Jesus, but believed he was a prophet and not the Son of God. Most people don't realize that some Muslims name their children Jesus or Mary because of their veneration of Jesus as a prophet. Geza Vermes, an Oxford University historian, writing from a Jewish point of view, believes Jesus was a man whose goal was simply to persuade the Jews to strive toward the kingdom of God by fulfilling the laws of the Torah (Jewish Old Testament Bible).[26]

The great Christian writer, C.S. Lewis, believed Jesus was more than just a prophet or great moral teacher. "We are faced, then, with a frightening alternative. This man we're talking about either was and is just what he said or else a lunatic, or something worse. It seems to me obvious that he wasn't either a lunatic or a fiend and consequently, however strange or terrifying or unlikely it may seem, I have to accept the view that he was and is God. God has landed on this enemy-occupied world in human form."[27]

Weren't most of America's founding fathers suspicious of the Catholic Church?

Yes, they were, and they probably had a right to be concerned. These great men wanted to create a new nation dedicated to liberty and religious freedom. They suspected "old world" religions and this especially included the mighty, universal Catholic Church, because of the Church's power and political influence. They may have worried that the church would restrict religious freedom.

Father John Courtney Murray contributed to the Catholic Church's *Dignitatis Humane,* a document issued at the close of the second Vatican Council in 1965.[28] Murray believed that the concept of religious freedom comes from sacred scripture and sacred tradition, "the treasury out of which the church continually brings forth new things that are in harmony with things that are old."

We hear stories of the early saints and martyrs, but now it seems like ancient history. Where are they today?

Today, Christians are martyred every day in Iraq and Syria, and in 2016 Pope Francis approved the beatification of 38 Albanian Catholics killed between 1945 and 1974 by their country's communist government, the world's first constitutionally established atheist state.[29]

A rather famous martyr of the 1940s was Maximilian Kolby. This Polish Franciscan priest volunteered to die in place of a fellow prisoner at the Auschwitz concentration camp in Poland. Pope John Paul II declared him to be "the patron saint of this difficult century."[30]

Of course, everyone is familiar with the work of Mother Teresa, a saint and holy person. Another important religious of the 20th century was Dietrich Bonhoeffer. This Lutheran pastor joined the German underground to fight Hitler. He was only 39 years old when he died and his books are extremely popular in both the religious and secular world. He was hanged by the Nazis in April, 1945.[31]

Haven't most Americans stopped going to church on a regular basis?

We've had a drop-off because of the "sinister" 60's, but according to Rodney Stark, Professor of Social Sciences at Baylor University, who is referenced in Part Three, Chapter 4, church attendance in the United States has held steady for the past 40 years.

Approximately 35% of Americans attend church weekly and this has not changed since 1974. Stark also reports that atheists make up only 5% of the world population and that religious belief increases, not decreases, the longer people attend school. So, religion is not just for the uneducated.[32]

Never fear, we'll be back! In October, 2018 a small article on page 18 of the *London Times* revealed that overall attendance, mid-week, at England's 42 cathedrals had increased by 160 percent since 2000! Interviews showed that stressed-out workers were looking for some "soul-food" during the week.[33]

Still rockin'? The Catholic Church is the only church in the United States expected to break the 100 million mark by the middle of this century. And while nearly half of all church membership was found in the northeastern United States in the 1950s, today it is spread out evenly across the country. Our Church continues to grow at a 1.5% annual rate while the US population growth rate is 0.9%.[34]

If this God of yours is so loving, what about the Holocaust? I have a Jewish friend who lost over 30 members of his extended family at Auschwitz. And what about the murder of 49 innocent people in Orlando, Florida in October, 2016, and the Synagogue murders in Pittsburgh in 2018?

We grieve for all victims of the Holocaust and are outraged by horrific actions of any kind. It's normal to blame God for bad things, but it's good to remember that if it were not for Judeo-Christian values, there would be no outrage over these deaths. The Romans thought of humans as animals and would have lost no sleep over the slaughter of gays or Jews. And Christians ranked high on their on their extermination list.

In fact, Christianity is the only religion that includes suffering in its Godhead. "The innocent sufferer, who was entirely human, stood before the relentlessness of fate and the injustice of nature, not as an impotent piece of humanity thrown to the winds, but as humanities great high priest."[35]

Jesus was nailed to a cross and knew what suffering was all about, but he wanted man to have free will. God intervention on demand is inconsistent with free will. Mankind remains free to make decisions, both good and bad. What we see as the end of a life, God may see as the beginning.

Another related question is why God takes away any of our loved ones, especially children. An Episcopalian priest lost his wife of 34 years and commented on how difficult it was to care for her over some 20 years. He questioned whether he could have continued much longer because we all have unknown limits as to what we can bear. He pointed out that even Jesus felt momentarily abandoned on the cross as any human would. "Someone can still ask, if nothing else, why this God has forsaken him. God gives, and God takes away. But he is still there."[36]

Your church pays homage to relics of saints and you hold out the shroud of Turin as proof of the resurrection. Hasn't science proved that the Shroud of Turin and relics of the cross could not have been from Christ?

Some Catholics and non-Catholics believe the Shroud of Turin to be Christ's burial cloth and there is well-documented evidence tracing the Shroud back to the time of Jesus by way of Constantinople, Turkey, and France. The research to date is impressive but the Church is taking a wait and see approach while encouraging more scientific research. For more information on this important and controversial subject, go to Appendix ll.

Relics? As to relics, perhaps you have held on to family heirlooms, photos, and other remembrances of people who were your role models. People you loved. People who cared for you. Perhaps it was your dear departed mother or "crazy" Uncle Larry. Maybe it was George Washington's wig. Is it wrong for individuals to hold a reverent attitude toward inspirational figures? What shall we call them? Hmm. What about relics? Do some people go overboard about relics? Probably. (Maybe the *Antique Road Show* is the answer—just kidding).

I understand that some popes were not exactly angels and let their power go to their heads.

Popes, too, are sinners. Peter, the first pope, denied Christ three times. Other popes have also proved to be only too human, letting power and politics interfere with their mission. It's important to realize that Catholics are bound by papal decrees only when the pope is speaking to all Catholics, from the chair of Saint Peter, on a matter of faith and morals. This rarely happens.

Martin Luther was also critical of the pope and at one point decided that the pope might be the Great Satan. But the pope continues to be a highly loved and respected world figure who still resides at the Vatican, the oldest continuing city – state institution in the history of the world. His independence allows for a world-view, one might say a heavenly view, which is less influenced by the fads and voices of regional and local cultures.

What about Luther? Wasn't he a great man?

We think Martin Luther was a sincere Catholic priest who wanted to help the Church. He learned that the Church was tolerating a small segment of clergy that raised money for the Vatican by selling indulgences (a "get out of jail card") that promised an early escape from Purgatory. Luther and other Catholic monks condemned this practice, but Luther expanded his complaints to include rejection of most Church teachings as well as the papal office. He wasn't the first priest to error in this manner, and he won't be the last.

About that time, Henry VIII of England renounced the Church in order to satisfy his own marital desires, and search for an heir to his throne. Germany had long resented Rome, massacring a Roman Legion in the days of the Roman Empire. Add the new-fangled printing press and the stage was set for the Reformation and the splitting of the Catholic Church.

Luther felt the pope wasn't necessary and thought man could be saved by reading the Bible directly rather than allowing the pope or Church historians, such as St. Augustine, St. Jerome, and Thomas Aquinas, help us understand the meaning of passages in the New Testament—which was written many years after Christ's death.

We believe that accepting everything in the Bible just as written, would limit our free will. Our free will lets us think, interpret, compare and look at the context or culture of the time. St. John's Gospel says that "you shall know the truth and the truth shall make you free."

St. Paul said "we can only see through a glass darkly." In other words, God gave us the ability (along with lots of help from the Holy Spirit) to shed light on the darkness. Most people don't realize that even the books of the Jewish Old Testament had differing versions and interpretations at the time of Christ.

People enjoy the freedom of everyone deciding what they think and feel about each word in the Bible, but it didn't take long before lots of people came up with contradictory interpretations. This put Martin Luther and other reformers in the position of having to establish church doctrine in order to guide Christians, much as the Roman Catholic Church had done for the 1500 years prior to Luther's protests. (The word Protestant comes from the word protest). At one point, Martin Luther even had to support German princes as leaders of his community in order to maintain a political structure for his new church.[37]

Protestants had to focus their energies on their new church's preaching, leaving little time for devotional prayers. As a result,

Protestants, even English Puritans, actually used versions of Roman Catholic devotions. The most famous example was the *Christian Directory or Exercise,* a work by the English Catholic priest, Robert Persons.[38]

David B. Barrett's research shows 33,820 denominations within Christianity.[39] The fact that there are 1.2 billion Catholics in the world does not prove that our papal-led Church is superior to any other church, but it does show that anti-papal protests were not accepted by everyone.

We also need to be open to ecumenical approaches (uniting under common beliefs) that will increase understanding and goodwill between all denominations. One of the difficulties with ecumenical outreach to other religious communities is the attitude of "ec YOU COME ical." We all want others to take the first step.[40]

Wouldn't we have more peace in the world without religion? Isn't it true that many people were killed during the Crusades and others have fought in the name of religion?

It is true that during the Crusades devout Catholics and others who were not so devout, took up arms to free the Holy Land from Muslim invaders. But the Crusades were mainly defensive in nature and were in response to centuries of attacks by Islamic forces. While there were some ruthless and evil crusaders, most of those who went on crusades were good Christians and behaved admirably. They went to join the pilgrimage to Jerusalem, after which they went home.[41]

A few thousand people were killed during the Crusades and perhaps as many as 2,000 in Inquisition trials. But just as in the Thirty Years' War, many conflicts counted as religious wars were not fought about religion. This includes Northern Ireland and the Israeli-Palestinian conflict. These disputes are influenced by ethnic disputes over self-determination and land."[42]

Here again, we can see that our church is a church of sinners, made up of people who may mean well, but who are not always following the gospel of Jesus Christ. Other churches can also fail from time to time. We sometimes forget that when the pilgrims landed at Plymouth Rock, they were Protestants escaping persecution in England from the Protestant Church.

Much of the time, political leaders used the Church to carry out their own wishes, but at times the Church itself allowed bad things to happen and could have done more to stop the use of physical coercion. Overall, the Christian religion has an outstanding record of preserving life. The Church has saved millions from starvation and abuse. Missionary workers and saints have reached out to people of every rank and station. Christians have led the way in the rejection of slavery.

Three-hundred-and-fifty-million have died from non-religious wars, including civilians who died from disease and famine, excluding abortion. Christians are responsible for less than 0.0128 of the total war deaths in world history. This is impressively low, but even though we are taking a scientific approach with our research in this book, morality is never a number count and killing, except in self-defense, is never acceptable.

Some historians claim that Pope Pius XII didn't do enough to protect Jews during WW II and that he conspired with the Nazis to protect the Catholic Church.

Some writers have criticized Pope Pius XII, but during World War II his office issued a binding condemnation of "the hatred which is now called anti-Semitism." Catholic bishops also condemned Nazism. Hermann Goering, second-in-command under Adolf Hitler, was aware of the silence of his own non-Catholic church compared to the attacks his Nazi party received from Catholic clergy.

In fact, the Catholic Church was probably more opposed to the Nazis than any other European group. Consequently, more Catholic clergy were killed than were ministers from other religious groups.[43] Golda Meier, who became prime minister of Israel, praised the pope and his efforts to help Jews during the war.

One heroic example of Church resistance is found in the actions of Clemens August Graf von Galen, bishop of Munster, Germany. In 1941, he gave homilies protesting Nazi criticism of Jews and called for a stop to the T4 program that murdered citizens classified by the state as "unproductive members of the national community." Children with epilepsy were included in this category of "lives unworthy of life." The Nazi's arrested the bishop and considered hanging him, but due to his efforts the T4 program was terminated.[44]

Perhaps the best evidence for Catholic resistance to the Nazi's comes from German Catholics in the pews. In the national election of July 1932, 56% of Germans in Protestant-dominated regions supported the Nazi's while only 21% supported the Third Reich in Catholic-dominated German regions.

Protestants had a mixed view of the Third Reich. The Institute for the Study and Eradication of Jewish Influence on German Church Life was inaugurated in1939 and launched in the Wartburg Castle where Martin Luther had translated the New Testament in 1521 – 22. The Institute played down the Old Testament of the Bible and believed that Christianity had to be purged of Jewishness. Martin Luther's 1543 tract, *On Jews and Their Lies*, stated that Christians had no moral obligation toward Jews.[45]

Could the pope have been more outspoken at times? Maybe. But 5000 Jews were rescued in the Vatican territory and if the pope had spoken out directly, these hidden Jews would have been found and deported. Also, when a Dutch Bishop denounced the Nazis', they doubled down by deporting all Jews baptized as Christians. [47]

It is often difficult to know the best response to terror, even in hindsight. The United States and its allies refused to bomb Jewish extermination camps because of fear of reprisal against other Jews. Our beloved president, Franklin Delano Roosevelt (FDR), turned back a ship of Jews seeking refuge that was anchored in New York Harbor, based on similar thinking. In October, 2018, Pope Francis declared Pope Pius XII a saint, based largely on his efforts to save thousands of Jews.

It's interesting that the same people who claim that the Catholic Church is not significant are the same folks who blame any and all of mankind's calamities on this "insignificant" institution. It occurs to the authors that one reason the Catholic Church is criticized for almost anything one can imagine is because it bravely comes forward with openly stated doctrines and beliefs. Our experience with leadership and company CEOs tells us that when someone is a transparent leader, they are easy targets for those who don't fully understand them or who are envious.

It's much safer to be vague and have shifting ideas and values. This way one can never be accused of being incorrect, rigid, or having an idea or rule that isn't popular at the current time. This is why politicians running for office hold off on revealing their true plans until the last moment. Fortunately, the church is above all that because its communications involve an eternal spiritual presence (God), and not slick political magazines, or news media shows on television.

Why didn't the church eliminate slavery? Why did it take until the 1800s before a non-religious U.S. government official abolished slavery in the United States?

You may hear that St. Paul tolerated slavery, and it is true that he stated: "Everyone should remain in the state in which he was called." This was because he believed that Jesus might be coming back in just a few years. Therefore, he lacked motivation to suggest changes to social injustices in the short time that he believed remained, even though he and other early Christians were sensitive to this issue.

Christianity, not the government, exerted most of the pressure to end slavery. The abolition of slavery is a good example of the limitations of secularism and atheism. These philosophies do not believe in the Bible or Judeo-Christian religions. As a result, they have no source outside of themselves and their limited logic, which is influenced by their current culture, to act against evil. What reason would they have? Atheists did not push for the end of slavery. Christians did. Government officials who opposed slavery were heavily influenced by Judeo-Christian values.[48]

This is also a good example of how a rigid interpretation of the Bible can lead to changes in biblical arguments supporting something like slavery, and why the literal, word-for-word approach to the New Testament and the Koran can be misleading. God gave us free will and the freedom to think and make use of our history and tradition.

The Catholic Church opposes divorce, but I hear that if you have enough money you can just whip off to Rome and get an annulment which lets you to remarry in the church.

This is hogwash. As psychologists, we have evaluated people's competency before trial. If one is not competent, one cannot be tried for any criminal act, including murder. If a person wasn't really competent or honest at the time of the marriage, then no marriage took place. This could include low intelligence, drug abuse, insincerity, etc. Perhaps we shouldn't use murder in the same breath as divorce, but there is one saying that has helped some married Catholics: "Murder yes, divorce no." (Ha).

Conclusion: We hope these responses to sensitive and often emotionally-based criticisms will give the reader a better understanding of an imperfect Church, one made up of sinners, but one that has done its best to follow the guidance of the Holy Spirit for over 2000 years. It's not easy to expose one's beliefs to public view, and to stand for unchanging values in a culture that expects compromise and even indulgence, but this is what gives our Church credence.

What about Darwin? Didn't he prove that all life can be understood entirely in natural and material ways and that man has been shaped by natural selection and other evolutionary processes? The world wasn't created in seven days, that's for sure.

Darwin, who was personally religious, admitted that of all the differences between man and lower animals, the moral sense of conscience was the most important. We believe that evolution has no explanation for the origin of the universe or its laws. Our Catholic position is that God is the creator of the universe, whereas the evolutionary debate is about how some of these changes came about.

Some folks worry that *The Book of Genesis* says God created the earth in six days, but St. Augustine saw this as just symbolic, and offered his interpretation 1500 years before Darwin came along.

Dr. Ben Carson, an internationally recognized neurosurgeon and the U.S. Secretary of Housing and Urban Development, is alleged to have said in response to an atheist who called him a moron for believing in God: "I believe I came from God and you believe you came from a monkey. You've convinced me you are right."

There are many other planets in the solar system. Maybe we're not so special?

It is extremely improbable that other planets can support life as we know it, *and it is also extremely improbable that our own planet can support life*. If gravity, along with electromagnetic and nuclear forces were off by a fraction of one in 100,000,000,000,000,000,000, no stars would have formed at all. And these forces were determined less than one millionth of a second after the Big Bang![49]

According to Eric Metaxis, the idea that the creation of our earth just happened would be like tossing a coin and having it come up heads a quintillion times in a row. "Our existence is a statistical and scientific virtual impossibility." He called this fine tuning.

Well-known atheist Christopher Hitchens said at one point: "Certainly, we atheists are asked about the best argument you come up against from the other side. I think everyone of us pick the fine tuning one as the most intriguing. You have to think about it; it is not trivial."[50]

We think the popularity of multi-universe theories shows how desperate religious critics are for answers. They seem to think that the existence of an infinite number of universes will make our universe less mysterious and less special. And just a footnote about our earlier reference to CERN'S large Hadron Collider: It's a good thing that scientists set the probability expectation high because subsequent teams of physicists reported that the bump on a graph signaling extra pairs of gamma rays was a statistical fluke.[51]

But won't science get there some day? Shouldn't we just wait and give science more time to disprove religion?

Here's the famous psychologist William James in 1896: "The command that we put a stopper on our heart, instincts, and courage and meanwhile act as if religion is not true—till doomsday—this command, I say, seems to me the queerest idol ever manufactured in the philosophic cave."[52]

You claim that the Church supports science, but didn't the church declare that the world was flat and the sun rotated around the earth?

The Catholic Church, and even the ancient Greeks, suspected the earth was round. They noticed that the hull of a ship sailing from shore would disappear before the top of the mast. It was also evident that during lunar eclipses the earth cast a circular shadow on the moon.

What about Galileo? Wasn't he tortured for his view that the earth moves around the sun?

Galileo wasn't tortured. He was, in fact, admired by the pope, who was an initial supporter of his scientific research. He was never charged with heresy, or placed in a dungeon, but he was confined to his residence.

Galileo had a feasible hypothesis about relative motion and tides, but had been unable to establish proof. At that time there was only shaky evidence for the theory that the earth moved around the sun. The pope asked Galileo to hold off on promoting this theory until proof could be established.

He was a good Catholic and agreed to this, but he embarrassed the pope by creating a conversation between two people in his book, one representing him and the other representing the pope. Galileo gave the pope's character the name "Simplicio," which means simple-minded. This was politically incorrect, to say the least, and the pope was not amused. Galileo also questioned passages from the Bible at a time when Protestant thinkers were claiming the Church did not take the Bible seriously enough.[53]

The system of Copernicus had been tolerated or ignored for nearly 80 years, and during that time the bitterest opponents had not been the Catholic Church, but Martin Luther and other reformers. Luther, of course, was insisting on a word-for-word interpretation of scripture.

Galileo lived out the remainder of his life in a small villa and his daughter got permission to leave her convent to stay with him. While his movements were limited, he did teach pupils, pursue studies, and receive visitors. Two of his visitors were the philosopher Thomas Hobbes and the poet John Milton.[54]

There you have it! Our inoculations couldn't begin to cover even a fraction of the ideas and activities surrounding our 2000-year-old Church. As a result, we sometimes felt we were being heavy-handed and "pounding nails" so to speak.

We hoped to offer direct and digestible responses, and didn't want our comments to be too vague. We hope the questions they raise will inspire you to check out other sources, whether it's *The Catechism of the Catholic Church, Catholic Answers Press*, googling, or visiting a good bookstore or library.

We hope you didn't have an allergic reaction to the needle—but please leave the protective tape on for a day or so.

PART EIGHT

Summing Up

Angels and Astronauts. Some learned folks still insist that faith and science are in conflict—but we think we know better.

Chapter 22

Angels and astronauts: an ape-man has no need for God.

As this book has demonstrated, science and religion are not always happy bed fellows. Science protests that religion is not scientifically provable and is therefore unscientific, (talk about circular reasoning) and religion complains that science is limited (ungodly) because it must break things into small parts in order to study them. Some Catholic theologians believe scientists sacrifice the big picture and ignore the wisdom of the ages.

Even though Christianity made science possible, there are still limits to what can be researched by Christians and non-Christians. Science can study problems and issues that lend themselves to tight control of most things that could mess up the research, in order that one outcome can be compared fairly to another, but our environment is pretty messy most of the time.

In fact, when it comes to brain research, Robert A. Burton, a leading neuro-physiologist, points out that the study of the brain is difficult because the brain is made up of 100 billion cells and a quadrillion synaptic connections (a message linking one part of the brain with another part of the brain). Even more limiting is the fact that "The brain is trying to study itself, and all of us, scientists and non-scientists, have biases that have developed out of our experiences. These experiences influence how we interpret scientific findings."[1]

E.O. Wilson, a theoretical biologist. Does he believe in the "Tarzan Theory" of human development? Wilson states that the brain is just a genetically hard-wired machine. Wendell Berry calls this the Tarzan Theory of the mind, because Barry believes a human raised entirely by apes would have only a rudimentary brain (unless they're named Tarzan and Jane, ha!).[2]

Jeffrey Hammond: "Anthropologists and psychologists tell us that we are not born knowing how to be human. This has to be taught and learned. The soul may well serve as a shorthand for our capacity to absorb this complicated bundle of lessons in the course of becoming fully human."[3]

What does current research tell us about what determines our personalities, physical traits and health? Michael Perri, Dean of the Clinical Psychology program at the University of Florida refutes the idea that biology is destiny. He points out that scientists thought we were on the cusp of understanding all human diseases with the completion of the Human Genome Project. He now concludes that we are all born with a genetic code, but the environment we live in can modify how our genes are expressed.[4]

New research shows just how vulnerable we humans are. We used to believe that the brain was largely complete before birth, but it now seems that humans need a fourth trimester, and this lasts until five or six months of age. This again reinforces the importance of early parental interaction with the child. These interactions establish lasting behavior patterns.[5]

Science does a good job of helping us to understand the natural world, but it has trouble focusing on things outside the natural world—things that can't be observed or tested, but Matt Emerson believes that science is faith-based too. He wrote about scientists' faith in a 1915 Einstein theory that led them, in 2016, to detect gravitational waves from 1.3 billion light years away. "Similar to the scientist's faith, our faith is informed by credible reason, nurtured by patient trust, and open to revision."[6]

Berry comments on these matters in his book *Life Is a Miracle: An Essay against Modern Superstition*: "Our daily lives are a mockery of our scientific pretensions. We are learning to know precisely the location of our genes, but significant numbers of us don't know the whereabouts of our children."[7]

Columnist Lee Gomes interviewed a group of people who believe that machines will synthesize into a new, super-intelligent life form. Gomes quotes a poem read at one of their conferences that describes an Aquarian age scene in which humans and other mammals frolic in a cybernetic meadow, watched over by machines of loving grace. Gomes states: "Those computer protectors sound a lot like the guardian angels my grade-school nuns told us about."[8]

"If we accept that knowledge is a finite island in a sea of inexhaustible mystery, then two corollaries follow: 1) The growth of the island does not diminish the sea's infinitude, and 2) The growth of the island increases the length of the shore along which we encounter mystery.[9]

The digital age has raised concern about too many details, too much prioritizing and excessive multitasking. Maybe an antidote can be found in the New Testament. Jesus entered a village where a woman named Martha welcomed him. Her sister Mary sat beside Jesus at his feet, listening to Him speak. Martha was burdened with all the serving and asked Jesus, "Do you not care that my sister has left me by myself to do the serving? Tell her to help me."

Luke 10:38–42 describes how Jesus replied to her: "Martha, Martha, you're anxious and worried about many things, when there is need of only one thing. Mary has chosen the better part, and it will not be taken from her."

Chapter 23

The Church's status today. Is it still rockin'? Is it still THE ROCK?"

How to wrap up a book on the validity of Christianity and the blessings of the Catholic Church? Marxism defines morality and religion as "phantoms formed in the human brain." Nietzsche believed morality was merely the herd instinct of the individual, and cultural anthropologists have emphasized the diversity of human life in various cultures. We like what political scientist James Q. Wilson (1931-2012) thought: that people are naturally endowed with certain moral sentiments, a disposition to make moral judgements. We think of this disposition as a defining quality of humanity.

"Man's moral sense is a small candle flame, casting vague and multiple shadows, flickering and sputtering in the strong winds of power and passion, greed and ideology. But brought close to the heart and cupped in one's hands, it dispels the darkness and warms the soul."[1]

As our research shows, the creation, history, and longevity of our Church is remarkable, and these findings are statistically significant, even from a secular, scientific, point of view.

The real power of the Church is found in a central truth: "that our lives are not first about ourselves. We can find true meaning in our lives only if we extend ourselves to others. Religion challenges us to live lives that extend beyond a narrow material and spiritual focus on ourselves. We can find greater meaning in living beyond ourselves as we negotiate our way in a complex age."[2]

So there you have it. A couple of non-clergy neuropsychologists with brain-behavior knowledge and clinical experience offer their perspective and viewpoint on the truths of the Church. We hope you enjoyed *A Catholic Survival Guide*. We ask you not to compare the Catholic Church with perfection, because the Church is made up of imperfect sinners.

Instead, please compare our Church to other political and religious institutions. Did any of these institutions begin with such meager resources and staffing, such minimal public relations, such mighty opposition—leading to martyrdom—last as long, and do as much good through charity and the uplifting of the mind and soul? We believe you have free will and can make up your own mind.

As we said in the Introduction, we're suggesting that you take the big jump and make the big splash and feel, smell, taste and experience religion. If you want spiritual and exotic, we've got that big time in the Catholic Church. If you like Halloween and spook shows, we've got the granddaddy of all spooks—the Holy Ghost…and more. We've got relics, incense, candles, exorcism, music, singing, paintings, sculpture, speaking in tongues, and don't forget Holy Bread!

Most of us are just people in the pews, but at the same time, who are the most intelligent and best balanced thinkers we know? The correct answer is the U.S. Supreme Court, and guess who's got more folks on the court than anyone else?

Did we present you with a well-balanced view of the history of Catholicism? No way! We wanted to give you an inoculation, and if you don't want it in the arm, we're willing to try some other—ah, ah, spot.

Let's allow another Catholic layperson to have the final thought. Peggy Noonan is a celebrated journalist and was a presidential speech writer for former President Ronald Reagan. She wrote an article on Christmases past and recalled a Christmas day when she was only 9 or 10 years old.

Peggy had badly wanted a desk, because she was already thinking of a career in the newspaper business. She prayed for a desk and on Christmas morning saw a rough, oblong piece of beige plywood stapled and nailed together. She wrote: "If you looked at it with imagination, it looked a lot like a desk." She got a kitchen chair, sat at the desk, closed her eyes, and thanked God.

"Then, suddenly, with my eyes closed, in my imagination, I saw it. Everything. There was a manger in the darkness and a man and woman. It was cold and there were stars in the sky and wise men came with their staffs and gazed in wonder. I never forgot it, of course, and in later years, teaching catechism classes, I said at the end all you have to do is remember: it's all true. It really happened. Just keep that in your mind."[3]

Appendix I

The Mathematical Formula Used in Part Three

This appendix presents the use of Bayes' Theorem to calculate our probability formulations.

Bayes devised a mathematical formula that takes into account an initial estimated probability of an event and then refines the probability each time additional information is available:

$$P(A|B) = \frac{P(B|A) * P(A)}{P(B)}$$

P(A|B) is the probability of event "A" happening if event "B" takes place.

P(B|A) is the probability of event "B" happening if event "A" takes place.

P(A) is the initial estimated probability of event "A" happening, before we refine our estimate with new information.

P(B) is the estimated probability of event "B" happening and can be further defined as being equal to:

$$[P(A) * P(B|A)] + [P(B|\bar{A} * (1-P(A))]$$

$P(B|\bar{A})$ is the probability of B happening if A does not happen.

Applying this equation to the four conditions below, and beginning with an estimated one in ten chance of success, we obtain the following:

1. The cultural and sociological conditions out of which the individual or venture evolves (what were the conditions in his neighborhood)?

We rate the probability on this factor at about a 20 to 1 chance of success. In other words, of those who are successful, only 1 in 20 would have such challenging cultural and sociological conditions. Assuming that one half of start-ups have challenging conditions such as this, we have the following:

$P(A) = 0.10$

$P(B|A) = 0.05$

$P(B|\bar{A}) = 0.55$

$P(A|B) = [(0.05) * (0.10)] / [(0.10 * 0.05) + (0.55 * 0.90)] = 0.01$

2. The amount of time the leader or leaders spend in establishing the venture or enterprise. The probability of something substantial starting this fast can be estimated at the 1 in 50 range. Taking into account factor one (above) our probability of success has already dropped to 0.01. We now must factor in the one in fifty likelihood of success for factor two. Assuming that one half of start-ups have similar time constraints, we have the following:

$P(A) = 0.01$

$P(B|A) = 0.02$

$P(B|\bar{A}) = 0.505$

$P(A|B) = [(0.02) * (0.01)] / [(0.01 * 0.02) + (0.505 * 0.99)] = 0.0004$

3. The amount of organized resistance to the individual, sect, or project, and the quality and degree of resistance—from simple objections to verbal harassment—to physical attacks and murder.

The fact that the early Christians survived again led us to an estimate of 1 in 50. Taking into account factors one and two, our probability of success has dropped to 0.0004. We now must factor in the one in fifty likelihood of success for factor three. Assuming that one in ten start-ups face similar organized resistance, we have the following:

$P(A) = 0.0004$

$P(B|A) = 0.02$

$P(B|\bar{A}) = 0.10$

$P(A|B) = [(0.02) * (0.0004)] / [(0.0004 * 0.02) + (0.10 * 0.9996)]$
$= 0.00008$

4. The public relations and media available to promote the new concept or person. We think there is only a 1 in 30 chance of successfully starting any venture with this level of marketing. Taking into account factors one through three, our probability of success has dropped to 0.00008. We now must factor in the one in thirty likelihood of success for factor four. Assuming that one half of start-ups face similar marketing limitations, we have the following:

$P(A) = 0.00008$

$P(B|A) = 0.033$

$P(B|\bar{A}) = 0.50$

$P(A|B) = [(0.033) * (0.00008)] / [(0.00008 * 0.033) + (0.50 * 0.99992)] = 0.00000533$

Using the initial expectation that starting up a new endeavor would have a one in ten chance of success, and then calculating the refined probability for each of the first four factors above, we find that the chances of finding success are 1 in 187,617, which is a probability of 0.00000533.

Appendix II

The Shroud of Turin

As discussed in Part three, there are at least three commonly used research methods. Most psychological studies set up an artificial, engineered situation where all variables (factors that could influence the study) can be tightly controlled. We saw this with Dr. Baumeister's study of self-control. A second method uses probability. The third method employs physical and observational science to analyze evidence. The many studies of the Shroud of Turin are a good example of this third approach.

Studies of the Shroud of Turin offer possible support for the resurrection of Jesus Christ. The shroud, a length of cloth bearing the image of a man, is believed by some Christians to be the burial shroud of Jesus. The Church has neither formally endorsed nor rejected the shroud, but in 1958 Pope Pius XII approved the image; Pope John Paul II called the shroud "a mirror of the Gospel."

The origins of the shroud and its images are subjects of debate among theologians and researchers. These arguments have found their way into popular magazines, television specials, and scientific publications. Attempts to show that the cloth is the authentic burial shroud of Jesus include chemical, biological, and medical forensics as well as optical image analysis.[1]

Sophisticated physical and observational sciences, including carbon dating and the use of a NASA image analyzer, verify that this image represents a 5'8" tall person who weighed approximately 155 pounds. Some researchers have used dust and pollen studies to trace the shroud back to the time of Christ and coins date it to the years A.D. 29-36.

Physical evidence can't be conclusive, but some scientists believe this information provides strong circumstantial evidence that this is the figure of Christ, perhaps at the moment of the resurrection. This evidence includes tracing the movement of the shroud from Israel, to Turkey, to France, where it was eventually discovered.

Max Fry, a criminologist, found pollen and dust samples that exist only in southern Israel, including Jerusalem and the Dead Sea. The image is a photo negative. This could mean that the shroud contains photo information 500 years before the invention of the photograph. NASA has used a 3-D analyzer and the image is three-dimensional. Even today, scientists are not sure how to *replicate* 3-D imagery of this type.[2]

There is also informed speculation that nuclear fusion within the burial site was responsible for the photo and the displacement of a several ton boulder covering the tomb. Since we don't know what Jesus looked like or have any other physiological information, there can be no comparison of blood type or other markers. Physicist Paola

Di Lazzaro is sympathetic with some of this evidence, but believes a miracle can't be investigated by the scientific method.

Law enforcement is rarely fortunate enough to have a witness to a crime. As a result, circumstantial evidence is often used to establish guilt or innocence. An example that made national headlines was the trial of O.J. Simpson, where the value of physical evidence, a glove, was still disputed despite the fact that it was found at the crime scene and not 2000 years earlier!

So where does that leave us? We're back to good old probability. Can we use Bayes' theorem to make a prediction based on probability? If a substantial number of scientists agreed to the physical evidence described above, we would venture a probability of 7 out of 10, or probably true. Remember the football field and the drone?

We would not expect most scientists to acknowledge this data, however, because they prefer not to deal with circumstantial evidence and certainly have no way to assess miracles. Many scientists have strongly held secular beliefs and acknowledging a religious breakthrough would disrupt their ego-driven status, which is earned through research and publications in scientific journals.

If these accumulated research results are accepted by only a small minority of scientists, it would reduce the odds to 2 out of 10, or probably not true. That would not mean that there is only 2 in 10 probability of the divinity of Jesus. It would only mean that this one piece of physical evidence, the shroud, does not clearly demonstrate the existence and importance of Jesus. Physical evidence is a strong scientific tool if it is valid, indisputable, and reliable. Establishing these parameters for the Shroud of Turin is most difficult at this time.

Appendix III

Seven Rules for Life

1. Treat others the same way you want them to treat you.

2. Go to church on a regular basis, pray every day, and go to confession; then you can relax about all the other stuff.

3. Let the Holy Spirit invade your brain to give you creativity and originality.

4. Help your parents and family, even if they bugged you a lot. Family is big, big, big.

5. It was the 10 *Commandments*, not the 10 suggestions!

6. Love the pope and his tradition, even if you think he's mistaken about something—or a couple of things.

7. Eat ice cream, but take care of your body.

Endnotes

Introduction
1. Kenneth L Woodward, *Getting Religion*, Convergent, 2016.
2. *Bad Religion, How We Became a Nation of Heretics*, Ross Douthat, Free Press, 2012.
3. *Concussion*, Sony Pictures: "Dr. Bennet Omalu Uncovers the Truth." 2017.
4. Robert P. George, "Houses of Worship," *The Wall Street Journal*, Oct. 14, 2016.
5. Nancy Jo Sales, *American Girls*, Knopf, 2016.

Part One: An Insider's Guide For People in the Pews.
Chapter 1:
1. Zossima Project, "Why do Catholics make the Sign of the Cross?" zossimaproject@gmail.com.
2. Zossima Project, "Lighting a Grotto Candle: What Does It Mean?" Religion and Ethics. *The Irish Rover*, October 6, 2016.
3. Christopher Theofanidis, "Rainbow Body," Tampa Bay Times Masterworks, Mahaffey Theater, St. Petersburg Florida, May 22, 2016.
4. Were You There? African-American spiritual, Matthew 27. 31-56. Unknown author, pre-1865.

Chapter 2:
1. Thomas Merton, *Opening the Bible*, The Liturgical press, 1970.
Chapter 3:
1. Harold G. Koenig, Duke University, 2018.
2. Trent Horn, *Why We're Catholic*, Catholic Answers Press, 2018.

Part Two: Psychology and Religion. Who are our Church leaders? Can they help us now?
Chapter 4:
1. 16PF® Questionnaire, *Institute for Personality and Ability Testing*, Inc., USA.
Chapter 6:
1. Ross Douthat, *Bad Religion, How We Became a Nation of Heretics*, Free Press, 2012.
2. Sydney M. Jourard, *The Transparent Self*, D. Van Nostrand Company, 1971.
3. *Catechism of the Catholic Church*, Catholic Book Publishing Company, 1994, page 360.
4. *Catechism of the Catholic Church*, Catholic Book Publishing Company, New York, 1994, page 430.
5. "Survey of Older Americans," Tampa Bay Times, December 25, 2015.
6. http://on.fb.me/1Vooler.
7. w.w.w.forbes.com/lists/2005/14/Revenue_1.html.
8. Eamon Duffy, *Ten Popes Who Shook the World*, Yale University Press, New Haven and London, 2011.
8b. Carl Rogers, University of Wisconsin Medical School, Grand Rounds, Feb. 1964.
9. Geeta Anand and Yaeyeon Woo, *The Wall Street Journal*, Nov. 27, 2015.
10. Niall Ferguson, Civilization, 2011, in William J Bennett's, *Tried by Fire*, Nelson books, 2016.

Part Three: Research Can Be Fun. Can Modern Science *Prove* Church Origins Were Inspired?
Chapter 8:
1. "Soccer," *Tampa Bay Times* wires, May 1, 2016.

2. "Mega Millions Jackpot Reaches 415 Million," Tampa Bay Times, July 2, 2016.

3. The Israel Museum, author visit, 2017. Josephus, *Jewish War II*, Viii, 12.

4. Carlo Rovelli, *Seven Brief Lessons On Physics*, Riverhead Books, 2014.

5. Robbert Dijkgraaf, "God Doesn't Play Dice," *The Wall Street Journal*, December 28, 2015.

6. Powerrankings.com.

7. Personal contact with Kelly Hicks.

Chapter 9:

1. Http://vitallongevity.utdallas.edu/knac/.

2. www.learning-theories.com/operant-conditioning-skinner.html.

3. Philip E. Tetlock and Dan Gardner, *Super Forecasting*, Crown publishers, 2015.

4. Roy F. Baumeister, psy.fsu/edu/faculty, "Self Control," 2011.

5. Acts, 37, *The New American Bible*, Consolidated Book Publishers, The Catholic Press, 1976.

Chapter 10:

1. John P Meier, *A Marginal Jew, Rethinking the Historical Jesus*, Doubleday 1991.

1b. John P Meier, *A Marginal Jew, Rethinking the Historical Jesus*, Doubleday 1991.

2. Keith Hopkins, "Christian Numbers and Their Implications," Journal of Early Christian Studies 6, no. 2, 1998.

3. Ken Curtis, "A Look at the Early Church," christianity.com.

4. Bishop Robert Barron, Word on Fire.org.

5. Chris Herring, "The NBA's Withering Heights," The Wall Street Journal.

6. Michael Lewis, *The Undoing Project*, W.W. Norton Company, 2017.

7. Nassim Taleb, *The Black Swan*, Random House, 2010.

8. Philip E Tetlock and Dan Gardner, *Super Forecasting*, Crown publishers,2015.

9. John P Meier, *A Marginal Jew, Rethinking the Historical Jesus*, Doubleday 1991.

10. Nagy, http://faith.nd.edu/s/2010/faith/social.

11. http://www.kaufmann.org/media research: entrepreneur.

12. Jason Nazar, Forbes, forbes.com. 2016.
13. smallbusinessnotes.com. (http://www.inc.com/thomas-koulopoulos/5-of-the-most-surprising-statistics-about-start-ups.html October 21, 2015) startups.
14. Chris Zook and James Allen, *The Founder's Mentality, Harvard Business Review* Press, June, 2016.
15. Kerry Brown and Simon van Nieuwenhuizen, *China, and the New Maoists*, Zed, 2016.
16. James Chapman, http://www.relevantmagazine.com/slices/bible.
17. Nate Silver, *The Signal and the Noise*, Penguin Books, 2012, Stephen D. Unwin, *The Probability of God*, Three Rivers Press, 2003.
18. "Value Judgments, The Best Offense Coaches," *Sports Illustrated*, March 23, 2016.
19. Christopher Ingraham, "Recent Deaths Don't Mean Parks Are Dangerous," *Tampa Bay Times*, August 14, 2015.

Chapter 11:
1. Rodney Stark *The Triumph of Faith*, ISI Books, 2015.
2. Ross Douthat, *Bad Religion*, Free Press, 2012.
3. *Bert Ehrman, The Triumph of Christianity*, Simon and Schuster, 2018.

Part Four: Do Church Teachings Reflect the Brain and Central Nervous System?
Chapter 12:
1. Jon Hassler, "Remembering Churches," *Why I am Still a Catholic*, Riverhead books, New York, 1998.
2. Alain de Botton, *Religion for Atheists*, Vintage Books, 2012.
3. New Testament: Mathew 9:9-13.
4. Edizione Piemme, *The Name of God is Mercy*, Spa, Milano, Penguin Random House, LLC. 2016.
5. www.telegraph.co.uk/news.
6. Gary Wills, *Why I Am a Catholic*, First Mariner Books, 2003.
7. "Art Under Attack: Histories of British Iconoclasm," Tate Britain Exhibition, 2 October, 2013 – 5 January, 2014.

Chapter 13:

1. Robert Ornstein, *The Right Mind: Making Sense of the Hemispheres,* Harcourt, Brace and Company, 1977.

2. Robert M. Sapolsky, *Behave,* Crown Publishers, 2016.

2b. The Pew Research Center, "demographic profiles of religious groups." 2017.

3. Jack Gallant, Gallant Lab, U.C. Berkeley, April, 2016.

4. Harry Harlow, *Motivational Forces Underlying Motivation,* 1954.

5. Erwin Chargaff, *Heraclitean Fire: Sketches from a Life in the 2000 before Nature,* Paul and Company, June, 1978.

6. Wendell Barry, *Life is a Miracle: An essay against modern superstition.* Counterpoint LLC, Mar 2000

7. Eric Bern, International Transactional Analysis Association, www. itaa – net.org, July 27, 2009.

Part Five: The Devil's laboratory. Media and Pop Psychology.
Chapter 14:

1. quoteinvestigator.com/2014/04/11.

2. www.wnd.com/2017/063.

3. Katayoun Kishi, "Christians Faced Widespread Harassment," Pew Research Center, Jun. 9, 2017.

4. Clare Ansberry, The Teenage Spiritual Crisis, *The Wall Street Journal,* Jun 14, 2017.

5. Max Bearak, "More Australians now identify as non-religious," *Washington Post,* Jul 2. 2017.

6. Joe Flint, "To Game TV Ratings, Don't Use Spell Check," *The Wall Street Journal,* Jul. 7, 2017.

7. Tampa Bay Times, 4A, June 17, 2018.

8. Nicholas Confessore, et. al., "Flynn's Distain for Limits Led to a Legal Mire," *The New York Times,* June 18, 2017.

9. "Fox News Drops Bill O'Reilly," Associated Press, *Tampa Bay Times,* Apr. 20, 2017.

10. Julia Dunn, Wall Street Journal, May 4, 2018.

Chapter 15:

1. John Berry, "Introduction to Testing," Dept. Clinical Psychology, University of Florida, 1966.
2. John Berry, "Introduction to Testing," Dept. Clinical Psychology, University of Florida, 1966.
3. Jordan Peterson, *12 Rules of Life*, Random House Canada, 2018.
4. Factcheck.org.
5. @politifact.com.
6. Political Fact Checking Under Fire.org.
7. cbsnews.com/news/.
8. Robert M Sapolsky, *Behave (The Biology of Humans)*, loc. 204, 2016. Penguin Group.
9. Robert M Sapolsky, *Behave (The Biology of Humans)*, page 8, 2016. Penguin Group.

Chapter 16:

1. Rodney Stark "The Rise of Christianity."
2. Aaron E. Carroll, Indiana University, March 13, 2018.
3. *Tampa Bay Times*, April 10, 2018.
4. Professor Mark Jacobson, Stanford University, November 2017.
5. William McGurn, the *Wall Street Journal*, May 1, 2018.
6. Associated Press, June, 2018.
7. Heather MacDonald, Manhattan Institute, October 10, 2017.
8. State of California vs. Dewayne Johnson, August 11, 2018.
9. Wall Street Journal, April 24, 2018.
10. Heidi Vogt, Wall Street Journal, April 25, 2018.
11. H. Gilbert Welch, *Dartmouth Institute*, November 2017.
12. Annals of Internal Medicine, 2014.
13. New York Times, September 9, 2018.
14. Brian Wansink, Cornell University, 2018.
15. Ornstein and Thomas, *The New York Times*, Dec. 9, 2018.

Chapter 17:

1. www.smithsonianmag.com/history/a-brief-history-of-the...
1b. Christopher Klein, "When America Despised the Irish," www.history.com.

2. James G. Blaine, conservapedia.com. 2017.

3. John F. Kennedy and Religion, Jfklibrary.org.

3b. Father Conroy, *Roll Call,* Jan 6, 2019.

4. www.townandcountrymag.com/society/politics/a23416484/brett..

4b. Eugene F. Rivers, Houses of Worship, *The Wall Street Journal,* Jan. 4, 2019.

4c. Gerald Baker, Review, The Wall Street Journal, Jan. 26-27, 2019.

5. irishecho.com/2011/02/78.

6. http://thesestonewalls.com/affidavit-of-rev-gordon-j-macrae/

7. http://www.themediareport.com/2013/05/21/ rev-gordon-macrae-case-facts/

8. The United States Conference of Catholic Bishops, March 28, 2016. Bishop accountability.org.

8b. Julie Asher, Catholic News Service, National Catholic Reporter, Feb. 11, 2019.

9. Mark Clayton, *The Christian Science Monitor,* March 21, 2002.

10. Charol Shakeshaft, "Educator Sexual Abuse," www.hofstra.org.

11. Tawnell D. Hobbs, U.S. Watch, *The Wall Street Journal,* May 26, 2017.

12. Elisabetta Povoledo, "Francis Sets Guidelines for Removing Bishops," *The New York Times,* June 5, 2016.

13. Sue Shellenbarger, "How Inaccurate Memories Can Be Good for You," *The Wall Street Journal,* July 27, 2016.

14. Elizabeth Loftus, Eye Witness, Harvard University Press.

15. Stacy Fince, www.SF gate, June 2003.

16. Tom Hoopes, Executive Director of the National Catholic Register. National Review Online, ttp://cbsn.ws/1dWh9Gz.

16b Patience Haggin, Suzanne Vranica, "YouTube Loses Viewers," *The Wall Street Journal,* Feb 21, 2019.

17. Timur Kuran, "Availability Cascades and Risk Regulation," University of Chicago Public Law & Legal Theory Working Paper, No. 181 (2007).

18. Mack Hicks, "Social Self and the Social Desirability Motive." Archives, University of Florida.

Chapter 18:

1. John Sides, Perspective: "White Christian America is Dying," Tampa Bay Times, August 28, 2016.
2. Can Prayer Determine the Will of God? http://www.religioustolerance. org/god_pra1.htm
3. Survey: Some Americans Actually Think Chocolate Milk Comes from Brown Cows. https://dairygood.org/content/2017/ survey-some-americans-think-chocolate-milk-comes-from-brown-cows.
4. https://www.washingtonpost.com/news/monkey-cage/ wp/2016/11/12there-may-have-been-shy-trump-supporters-after-all/?utm_term=49b2afd65e4c.
5. Mack Hicks, *Social Self and the Social Desirability Motive*, University of Florida Archives.

Part Six: Undressing the Devil.
Chapter 19:

1. Robert M. Sapolsky, *Behave, The Biology of Humans—Our Best and Worst*, 2017.
1b. Steven Pinker, Enlightenment Now, Viking, Feb. 2018.
1c. Max Roser, Our World in Data, website, 2019.
2. Ara Norenzayan, *Big Gods*, Aug 2015.
3. Anna Maxted, Family and Features, *The Daily Telegraph*, February 2, 2017.
4. David McClelland, *Need for Affiliation, 1961.*
5. Robert Sapolsky, *Behave, The Biology of Humans—Our Best and Worst*, 2017.
6. Commentary: mack-hicks.com
7. Daphna Joel of Tel Aviv University, *Trends in Cognitive Sciences and Philosophical Transactions of the Royal Society.*
8. Mack Hicks, *Parent, Child, and Community*, Nelson Hall Publishers.
9. www.terrapsych.com.
10. Karl Marx: *A Nineteenth Century Life*, Johnathan Sperber Mar. 2014.
11. Harry Harlow, *A Science Odyssey*, People and Answers, pbs.org.

Chapter 20:
1. Mersenne: https://primes.utm.edu/mersenne/.
2. Ricci: Matteo-Ricci, britannica.com.
2b. Tim Peterson, *The CONNECTION To Your Community*, Jan.4, 2019.
3. Lemaitre:www.pbs.org/wgbh.
4. *The Catechism of the Catholic Church*, Catholic Book Publishing Company New York, New York, 1992.
4b. "An Astronomer's View of the Christmas Sky," Kyle Peterson, WSJ, Dec. 23, 2018.
5. Jackie Goldman. Individual Frustration Tolerance in Rats, University of Florida, Archives, 1985.
6. John Barry, "A Photo Album of the Soul," *Tampa Bay Times*, June 14, 2008.
7. news.bbc.co.uk/onthisday/hi/dates/stories/June/2/newsid_3972000/...
8. Robert Persons S.J. *The Christian Directory (1582) The First Booke of Christian Exercise, Appertaining to Resolution*, edited by Victor Houliston, Brill, 1998.
9. *The Journal of Sex Research*, Vol 51, 2014.
10. *Psychology Today*, January 14, 2013.
10b. Dennis Prager, *The Rational Bible*, Regnery Press, 2018.
11. *The Psychological Monitor Archives* are no longer available. Aug., 2018.
12. Harry Harlow, *A Science Odyssey*, People and Answers, pbs.org.

Part Seven: Inoculation —— "God is Dead."
Chapter 21:
1. Entertainment, a free news feature on aol.com.
2. Diep Tran, "You can go your own way." Sunday Style, New York Times, Dec 27, 2015.
3. Innosanto Nagara, Triangle Square, Books for Young Readers (www.7stories.com)
4. Trent Horn, *Why We're Catholic*, Catholic Answers Press, 2017.
5. Friedrich Nietzsche, *Thus Spoke Zarathustra*, Sterling Publishers, 2012.
6. Personal contact with authors, July, 2016.
7. John Waters, *Beyond Consolation*, Continuum, 2010.

8. american grace.org.
9. Peter J Rubinstein, Houses of Worship, "Thinking About Charity on Black Friday," *The Wall Street Journal,* November 25, 2016.
10. Roy F. Baumeister, "Self Control," psy.fsu/edu/faculty, 2011.
11. Charlotte Allen, Houses of Worship, "Ben-Hur's Watered-Down Christianity," *The Wall Street Journal,* August 26, 2016.
12. http://www.usccb.org//bible/readings/072215.cfm.
13. Pope Benedict XVI. *Light of the World, Ignatius Press, 2010.*
14. Charlie Brown, *"This Peculiar Marriage," Why I Am Still a Catholic,* Continuum Books, 2005.
15. www.gallup.com/poll/154799.
16. William McGurn, *"A Peddler's Words," Why I Am Still a Catholic,* Riverhead books, 1998.
17. Neil Scolding, "On the Sidelines of a Culture of Death, Why I Am Still a Catholic, Continuum Books, 2006.
18. Keith L Moore, *The Developing Human: Clinically Oriented Embryology,* Ninth Edition. Saunders, 2011.
19. Mary Cunningham Agee, *His Way, Truth, and Life, Why I Am Still a Catholic,* Riverhead books, 1998.
20. John Russell, Gospel Reflection from Notre Dame, faith@nd.edu, 2015.
21. Thomas X.F. Noble, *Popes and the Papacy: A History,* The Teaching Company, 2006.
22. *Soul-Searching: The Religious and Spiritual Lives of American Teenagers.* New York. Oxford University Press 2005.
23. Amy Schill, "Gospel Reflections from Notre Dame," April 27, 2016.
24. David Meyers, The Pursuit of Happiness, 1993.
25. *Bad Religion (How We Became a Nation of Heretics,* Free Press 2012.
26. Geza Vermes, *The Authentic Gospel of Jesus,* Penguin books, 2002.
27. CS Lewis, Fellow of Magdalen College, Oxford, *The Case for Christianity, Radio Broadcast Talks,* The McMillan Company, 1946.
28. www.vatican.va/.../vat-i¬_decl¬19651207_dignitatis humanae_en.html.
29. Romeo Gurakuqi, Pope Francis and Martyrs to Communism, "Houses of Worship," *The Wall Street Journal,* May 20, 2016.

30. Andre Frossard, *Forget Not Love, The Passion of Maximilian Kolby*, Ignatius Press, 1987.

31. *The Cost of Discipleship*, Dietrich Bonhoeffer, Simon & Schuster, 1959.

32. Rodney Stark, *The Triumph of Faith*, ISI books, Intercollegiate Studies Institute, 2015, "General Social Surveys, Baylor Religion Survey."

33. *London Times*, Oct. 2018.

34. Clarence Thomas, "Notable and Quotable," The Wall Street Journal, May 17, 2016.

35. N. Wilson, Houses of Worship, "The Book of Job's Big Question," The Wall Street Journal, June 24, 2016.

36. Victor Lee Austin, "The God Who Took Away My Wife," Houses of Worship, *The Wall Street Journal*, September 16, 2016.

37. Reformation, *Europe's House Divided, 1490-1700*, Diarmaid Macculloch, Folio Society, London, 2003.

38. Diarmaid Macculloch, *Reformation, Europe's House Divided 1490 – 1700*, *pg. 627*, Folio Society, London, 2013).

39. Oxford University Press (2001).

40. Fr. Tony Nye SJ, Jesuit Church of the Immaculate Conception, Farm Street, Jan 22, 2017.

41. Islam, Andrew Bieszad, *20 Answers, Catholic Answers*, 2015.

42. Dinesh D'Souza, *What's So Great About Christianity*, Regnery Publishing, 2007.

43. Michael Burleigh, *Sacred Causes, The Clash of Religion and Politics from the Great War to the War on Terror*, HarperCollins Publishers, 2007.

44. Sohrab Ahmari, Houses of Worship, "The Bishop Who Took On the Fuhrer," *The Wall Street Journal*, May 19, 2017.

45. Alec Ryrie, *Protestants*, Viking, 2017, 266-268.

46. Benedict XVI, *Light of the World, The Pope the Church and the Signs of Times*, Ignatius Press, 2010.

47. Eamon Duffy, *Ten Popes Who Shook the World*, Yale University Press, 2011.

48. Dinesh D'Souza, *What's So Great About Christianity* Regnery Publishing, Inc. 2007.

49. Eric Metaxis, *Miracles*, Penguin – Random House, 2015.

50. Eric Metaxis, "*Are Atheists Afraid of God?*" Houses of Worship, *The Wall Street Journal*, June 3, 2016.

51. Dennis Overbye, "Secret to The Universe, That Was Really Just a Blip," *New York Times International* August 6, 2006.

52. William James, "The Will to Believe," Harvard Lecture, 1896. Gertrude Himmelfarb, Books, "The Once-Born and the Twice-Born," *The Wall Street Journal*, September 29, 20012.

53. Dinesh D'Souza, *What's So Great About Christianity*, Regnery Publishing, 2007.

54. www.sparknotes.com/biography/Galilao/sec.9.

Part Eight: Summing Up.
Chapter 22:

1. Richard A. Burton, *A Skeptic's Guide to the Mind: What Neuroscience Can and Cannot Tell Us about Ourselves*. St. Martin's Press, 2013.

2. Edward O. Wilson, Consilience: *The Unity of Knowledge*, Vintage, 1999, New York.

3. Jeffrey Hammond, lost souls, Notre Dame Magazine, Spring, 2005.

4. Michael Perry, PHHP News, University of Florida. Fall, 2016.

5. Mercedes Paredes, the Journal of Science, October, 2016.

6. Matt Emerson, *Why Faith? A Journey of Discovery*, Paulist Press, 2016.

7. Wendell Barry, *Life is a Miracle: an essay against modern superstition*, Counterpoint, Berkeley California, 2001.

8. Lee Gomes, "The Singular Question of Human Versus Machine Has a Spiritual Side," *The Wall Street Journal*, December 19, 2007.

9. Chet Raymo, "Machines vs. Humanity," *Notre Dame Magazine*, Spring, 2002.

Chapter 23:

1. James Q. Wilson, "What is Moral and How Do We Know it?" *Commentary Magazine*, June,1993.

2. Nicholas Burns, *Why I Am Still a Catholic*, Riverhead books, New York, 1998.

3. Peggy Noonan, *The Wall Street Journal*, December 25, 2015.

Appendix II: The Shroud of Turin.

1. J. Michael Fischer, http://newgeology.us/presentation24.html
2. http://www.cnn.com/videos/tv/2015/02/25/finding-jesus-shroud-1.cnn.

Acknowledgements

The authors would like to thank Steve Keteltas for his present and past efforts as an editor and friend who offered critical insight and constructive criticism. A poet, musician, writer, and dancer, his support is special.

Thanks also to Ghislain Viau at Creative Publishing Book Design. His cover and design work is creative and outstanding. He is prompt and efficient. A real pro. www.creativepublishingdesign.com

Hats off to Bill Applegate of the Catholic Press Association for taking his valuable time to teach some newcomers about Catholic publishing.

Deb Kelly has assisted both authors for many years with media placement and publishing production. She is highly recommended. thewriteonecs@aol.com

Sharon Withers was instrumental in sorting out the notes and references that Mack Hicks managed to leave in a jumbled mess. Thanks for your analysis, energy, and determination, Sharon.

Tom Bostock was most helpful in editing portions of the final manuscript. He was prompt, reliable, and rigorous with his corrections and suggestions. tbosticwriter@gmail.com

About the Authors

Dr. Andy Hicks is a scientist-practitioner who was trained at Vanderbilt University and the University of Florida Department of Clinical and Health Psychology, Shands Hospital. He has been a Clinical Neuropsychologist and Director of Assessment and Research since 1988.

Dr. Hicks has published in *Neuropsychology and Cognition*, the *Southern Medical Journal*, and the *Journal of Clinical and Consulting Psychology* and has been a consultant to numerous community and professional programs. He has been awarded for outstanding contributions to the profession of psychology, and in 2013 was designated a Distinguished Psychologist.

Dr. Mack Hicks is a scientist-practitioner who trained at the University of Florida, and the University of Wisconsin. Hicks was lead scientist on a grant from the National Institute of Health. He practiced for over 30 years in the field of child and adolescent neuropsychology and opened the first school for dyslexics in the United Kingdom. He founded schools in the U.S. to deal with learning disabilities, attention deficit disorder, and autism.

Nonfiction works include: *Parent, Child, and Community* (Nelson Hall Publishers), *The Digital Pandemic* (New Horizon Press), and *The Elephant in the Classroom.* Dr. Hicks writes articles for the *Psychology Today Magazine* website. His personal website is mack-hicks.com.

CPSIA information can be obtained
at www.ICGtesting.com
Printed in the USA
FFHW010117250519
52634329-58138FF

9 780971 258747